5

THE LONELY SEA

THE LONELY SEA
YVETTE ALLUM

PIER
9

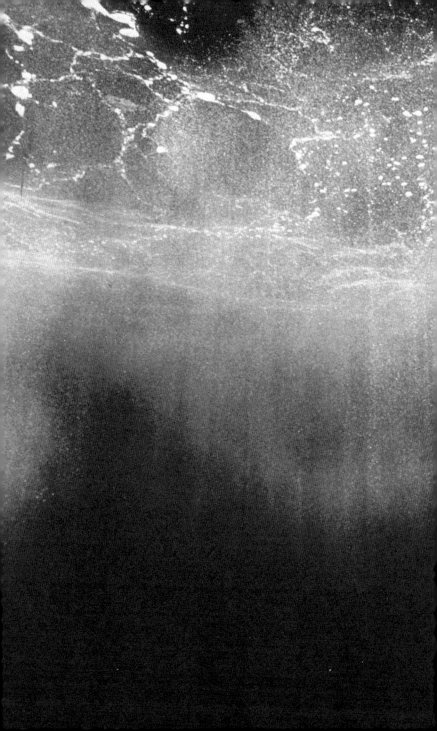

FOR RONNIE, MADELAINE AND SOPHIE

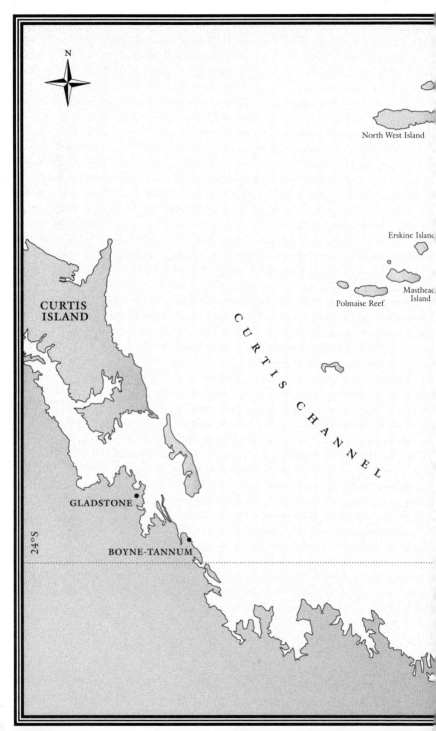

152°E

C A P R I C O R N   C H A N N E L

Wilson Island

Wreck Island

Heron Island

Wistari
Reef

One Tree Island

CAPRICORN GROUP

**BUNKER
GROUP**

24°S

152°E

PREFACE

On 5 January 1983, a pack of excited reporters descended upon Gladstone District Hospital, cameras, tape recorders and notebooks in hand, primed for an interview that smelled distinctly like front-page news. They waited impatiently in the reception area until a nurse came out to inform them that the interviews would have to be conducted in two shifts.

The first twenty or so were ushered into a wardroom where they crowded around a hospital bed. Over the previous two days, there had been brief reports indicating hopes were fading for a woman who went missing while diving on the Great Barrier Reef. At that stage, the story rated only a small mention.

Now, lying in the bed in front of them was the woman in question: Sue Dockar, her face and wrists badly sunburned, her lips cracked and swollen, her honey blond hair bleached white from salt and sun. That morning she had been spotted and rescued by a local helicopter pilot after spending forty-six hours in heavy seas and a further twenty-four on a tiny coral cay without food or water. Miracle stuff.

The questions flew. The cameras clicked and flashed. In the midst of the mayhem a shy, war-weary Sue Dockar struggled to find the words to describe her three days of hell.

'Did you see any sharks?'

'Yes, but they went away after a while.'

'What were you doing out there?'

'I was competing in a spearfishing competition.'

'What did you think about during the night?'

'My husband Greg and everybody else on shore.'

'What kept you going?'

'I didn't want to die. I just didn't want to die.'

It was all very cordial. After forty minutes the first group of reporters left and the second group came in. They asked the same questions. She gave the same answers. Forty minutes later and they were off to file their stories.

The following morning, Sue and her remarkable story of courage and endurance made front-page news around Australia. 'SUE DOCKAR — WONDER WOMAN OF THE SEA', 'WOMAN DIVER ALIVE!' read the headlines.

A news story might run for a few days, maybe a few weeks, ebbing or flowing in priority, depending on the images and controversy that follows. Disaster, scandal, tragedy, triumph. Clipped stories, the essential elements of which are compounded into the first fifty words for those busy individuals who want to be informed of the facts and the gossip but care little for the detail.

And then the story disappears. It becomes old news — archival footage in the fast-paced media world where the here and now rules supreme.

It is a comfortable, clinical environment where the consumer can experience humanity's highs, lows, horrors and hysteria at a safe distance, switching from one item to the next with the turn of a page or the click of a button. For those under the spotlight there is a tidal wave of attention, prying lenses and questions, culminating in neatly packaged exposés, starkly displaying their most vulnerable moments of grief, anger, jubilation and despair alongside advertisements for automobiles and cures for impotence.

What is not reported are the subtle characteristics, circumstances and conditions that converge to create history, cause accidents, make a person react in one way rather than another. These are the seeds of the thousand 'what ifs' and 'if onlys' that bemuse coroners and investigators, and forever haunt the quiet times of those touched by crime or tragedy.

This is perhaps most evident where a person is missing, presumed dead. Then, the true story and the answers to those subtle but important questions may be forever locked away in the minds of the victim and those party to their disappearance.

But sometimes the victim comes back. Sometimes, those given up for dead return and have the opportunity to consider these questions for themselves.

It took a couple of weeks for the Sue Dockar story to die down, during which time Sue and her husband Greg returned to their home in the Sydney suburbs. A week later, the press had turned their attention to something else. It was all over.

I didn't know Sue back then. But over the years her story matured into a favoured spearfishing yarn, told over a cold beer by those in the know and those who were there. It suited the image of the tight-knit spearfishing community, highlighting the tough individualistic nature of the sport, positively oozing machismo — except that in this case the hero wore a bikini.

I was present at one such recital and found myself fascinated as the storyteller relived the ordeal on Sue's behalf. He told of her encounters with sharks, of how she had floated around at night and seen strange lights in the sea and, of course, of her triumphant return to Gladstone where she discharged herself from hospital after just one night. In my mind I built up an image of Sue Dockar: she would be brash, even rude on occasion. She strode rather than walked and carried her head high, with the clichéd 'mane of blond hair' billowing in the wind. She would drive her own boat, catch her own dinner and could probably take the cap off a beer bottle with her teeth.

Eventually I met Sue, eight years after her ordeal, and this image was shattered. The Sue Dockar I was introduced to was a quiet, rather timid woman who, at the time, was nursing a baby on her hip. Her hair was blond, but short and permed, and she wore glasses slightly thicker than my own. She didn't stride and, while she could drive a boat, she preferred a small glass of shandy to a bottle of beer.

When I asked about her ordeal she looked rather embarrassed. What did I want to know? she asked. I said I would like to write up the story. Sue thought about this for a while and then said, 'OK, but all I did was float. I don't know how much you can write about that'.

BLUEWATER

Even in the diving world we are regarded as eccentric and perhaps on the lunatic fringe. Who are these people on the far outside of the kelp beds, in camouflage wetsuits, avoiding other divers and evasive in their answers of where they were and what they were doing?

Bob Donnell, United States Spearfishing Champion 1969

Bluewater came through two weeks back. It swept away the green turbid seas of winter exiling the cold and gloom, leaving the Sydney coastline bathed in warm, clear heaven. Summer had finally arrived, brought down from Queensland courtesy of the East Australian Current. Getting an interview with any skindiver was going to be hard work in these conditions. But I was in luck. Ray Inkpen and Allan Moore were diving in Sunday's spearfishing competition. They had space for me on their boat as long as I didn't throw up too much. 'OK', I said. '8.30 am, the picnic shelter, Gunnamatta Bay.'

To be quite honest I deplore competition fishing of any kind. But competition is the essence of this story. It is what kept some people together and drove others apart. So I arrived early, put on my swimmers, wetsuit long john and sunscreen and sat under a corrugated iron picnic shelter perched on top of a grassy slope. A small flotilla of boats was assembling on the sandy foreshore below. They ranged from scraggy runabouts to sleek twin-engine monsters, but there were certain common themes. Most were geared up for speed not comfort, with engines at maximum capacity for the size of the vessel. Luxuries such as seats had been removed. In their place were plastic fish boxes and a loose assortment of diving masks and fins, weight belts and spearguns. Wetsuit-clad men and the occasional woman milled around the boats, shouting hellos and catching up with their mates. To the uninitiated, what draws the eye is the colour of some wetsuits. Not the standard black, red or blue, but the brown-green mottle of army camouflage.

They were there to compete for the coveted Alliman Shield, a memorial trophy in honour of champion spearfisherman Curley Alliman, who drowned off Sydney's Coogee Beach in 1956. Weather permitting, the competition is held on the first Sunday of each month. The diver who accumulates the most points over the year takes the shield for their club. It was the first Sunday in December 1997 — the last Alliman competition before the national spearfishing championships. Divers from all the Sydney clubs had turned out — San Souci, St George, Mosman Whalers, North Shore.

I spied Allan and Ray among a knot of divers making their way up the hill. It was hard not to notice Allan in the crowd. He was tall and handsome. If he starred in a movie he would be the stranger who rode in on a white horse and saved the town. Ray, a good forearm shorter than Allan, had the tighter, more muscled build of a boxer. Even his thick hair stood to attention like a barber's brush. At the time Ray ran a team of powder monkeys who blasted sandstone from a quarry west of Sydney. They never used less than 10 tonnes of explosives at any one time. He had an interesting sense of humour.

'You made it then', said Ray with a smile.

'Wouldn't miss it.'

We discussed the tides, the sea conditions and the nor'easter due to hit Sydney that afternoon. All things considered the plan was to head out of the bay and turn north — nothing too serious. Nothing too serious was good. There were people in this crowd who took the word serious to extremes. One guy had a reputation for driving his boat so hard that he regularly punched holes in its fibreglass hull. Another, in his haste to beat a rival boat to a prime fishing site, drove full bore into a heavy sea, breaking the ribs of two of his passengers in the process. There were plenty more tales of boats that had gone too close to the cliffs and been swamped or rolled, and divers with prized fish on their line who had prodded away inquisitive sharks with their speargun as they swam the kilometre or so into shore — all in the name of competition. Officially, such practices were frowned upon. Officially.

By 8.45 around sixty divers had converged on the picnic shelter, merging into an anonymous mass of neoprene, sweat, salt and flat-toned diving talk. A marshal from each club stood dutifully with a sign-on sheet in hand, taking down the names of team members as they arrived. I followed Ray and Allan in search of Merv Sheehan, the president, and that morning, the marshal for St George Spearfishing Club.

The secret to finding Merv was to look for a huddle or listen for an argument. Merv was usually in the middle of one or both. True to form we located the huddle and found Merv who was simultaneously administering the sign-on, settling some pre-comp dispute and arranging a place on someone's boat for a guy who had just arrived in Sydney from up the coast.

Merv was a large man in his sixties with that combination of white hair, fat stomach and booming voice that makes you think of Father Christmas — except that this Father Christmas wore a wetsuit and carried a clipboard. He was a controversial character, a gun spearo in his day with a temper to match. The years had weathered and mellowed him, tumbling him like waves roll a pebble on a beach. But the old Merv was still in there. He still speared, still doggedly stood his ground when the odds were stacked against him, still commanded respect among a group of people who judge themselves and their peers against a monthly score sheet. Love him or hate him, they all agreed that spearfishing was Merv's life. Some of those taking part in the Alliman had never known spearfishing without Merv.

He looked up over his glasses and nodded hello to Ray and Allan. Then he turned to me.

'Good to see you', he said. 'Are you fishing?'

Before I had time to answer, Merv's attention had been diverted. It was five minutes to nine and the competitors were gravitating to a large square of grass roped off to form the starting pen. Merv gathered up his papers and stopwatch and ambled out to the crowd. He mounted his podium, a conveniently placed esky, and suddenly there was quiet.

'It is now four minutes to nine — everybody hear that?' he said.

There was a low mumble of confirmation.

'Sign-off is one o'clock sharp. No exceptions.'

Everyone knew the rules but Merv went through them anyway: each diver was only allowed to weigh in one fish of each species listed on the score sheet and each fish had to be over a specified weight and/or length. Any diver who failed to get back to the pen by 1 pm would be disqualified.

As Merv counted down the time competitors started pairing up with their mates, preparing to make the bolt down the hill to their boats. One minute. Thirty seconds. Fifteen seconds. Men started to jostle at the front of the pen. 'Three, two, one!' The whistle blew. For the next few minutes the scene descended into mayhem. Competitors raced down the slope towards the beach and scrambled aboard their boats, hurriedly pulling up anchors and ripping their engines into action. But not everyone took proceedings so seriously. Ray and Allan hung at the back of the pack.

'Let them go', said Ray.

By the time we reached the beach the last of the boats were leaving. We waded out to a 3.7 metre single engine aluminium hull, affectionately referred to as the tinnie. Ray and I clambered in while Allan pushed the boat out to deeper water. Then Ray gave the crank cord a swift pull and the engine roared into life, belching a cloud of two-stroke into the morning air.

It's an odd game, spearfishing. While anglers cast their line from the safety of a wharf or boat, spearos slip beneath the waves and into another world. They may spend hours in the water, watching, waiting, working on gut instincts and ignoring the urge to breathe, the only limits on depth and endurance being those the diver sets themselves.

Apart from the obvious mask, snorkel and fins the tools of the trade are a handspear or speargun and a rigline. While handspears are confined to a rod-like design, guns come in all shapes and sizes, from short weapons for kelp beds and caves, to 2 metre long shafts for hunting tuna, Spanish mackerel and marlin. Both types work on the same principle as the schoolyard catapult, with the spear placed in a taut rubber sling which, when triggered, hurls it towards its target. The range of the weapon depends on the tension of the sling — the greater the tension, the further and faster the spear will be propelled.

The rigline, about 18 to 30 metres long, runs from the diver's gun to a small buoy on the surface. The line is threaded through the gills of speared fish and wave movement gradually draws the fish back, away from the diver. Before that, most divers hooked their catch onto a waist belt, but the practice went out of vogue after South Australian spearfisherman, Rodney Fox, was bitten nearly in half by a white pointer, supposedly attracted by the fish dangling from his torso. Astonishingly, Fox survived.

Plenty of people dabble with spearfishing while on holiday or when the weather looks good or the cupboard is bare. But competitive spearfishing is different. In this world, a person's standing is based upon how deep they can dive, what fish they have caught, what sea conditions they can handle. It is a bloodsport — a sport that draws and perpetuates a certain type of diver, one characterized by stubborn self-reliance and, however deeply it is hidden, an extremely competitive streak.

To many they are Hemingway characters in a New Age world, still chasing the thrill of the kill even though wild fish stocks are disappearing fast. For their part spearfishers regard their critics as hypocrites, pointing out that the same people who condemn spearfishing fiercely defend their right to line fish with live bait or consume seafood trawled indiscriminately from the ocean floor; that our politicians argue while Australia, one of the driest continents on earth, pours billions of litres of sewage and stormwater run-off into the ocean every year.

Popularity is not what competitive spearfishing is about. It's about dropping over the side of a boat in the middle of nowhere and diving down into blue nothing. It's about taking on your prey in its own world with only your speargun, your wits and a lungful of air. It's about white-knuckle boat rides on the open sea, where the props leave the water and engines scream. It's about a cold beer with your mates and tales of the one that got away. But most of all, when that whistle blows, it's about winning.

The pack headed out from the park towards a tight channel through Gunnamatta Bay's notorious sandbanks to Port Hacking. As they came clear of the channel the boats surged forward, their bows rising, salt spray flying as they planed across the waves. Gradually the movement of the water changed from the flat calm of the bay to the long undulating swell of the open sea. The boats fanned out. Some went north up the Sydney coast towards Long Bay, Wedding Cake Island and Bondi. Others went south towards Wattamolla. They were heading for favoured fishing grounds, rock outcrops and distant reefs.

Our tinnie flew across the swell, the aluminium hull slamming from one wave to the next. Up past Cronulla Beach and on towards

Malabar — a ruggedly beautiful stretch of coast, a collage of sandstone, scrubland and beaches, made all the more amazing by its proximity to Sydney's smog-engulfed hub. Allan and I gripped the tinnie's forward gunwales while Ray kept the throttle down. Salt spray drenched our faces and stung our eyes. I looked across to Ray and Allan. They wore grins as big as Halloween pumpkins.

Just as the trip was starting to get painful we reached the cliffs outside Malabar Bay. Perched on top of the sandstone cliffs is a small village, a sprawling golf course, a hospital, a rifle range, Long Bay Gaol (until recently the largest prison in New South Wales) and a sewage treatment works. For more than a century, the treatment works poured tonnes of Sydney's effluent out from the cliffs each day. Drive through Malabar in those days on a hot afternoon with onshore winds and the stench was overpowering. From an aquatic perspective it had to be one of the most putrid dives in Australia.

In 1994 the outfall was extended 2 kilometres offshore. The massive brown slick that had cursed Malabar for more than a century slowly petered into nothing. Local real estate values soared and people started diving around the mouth of the old outfall tunnel that had been carved through the cliffs.

The 1.5 by 1.5 metre wide outfall mouth was in less than 10 metres depth of water. The first thing divers discovered was that anyone unfortunate enough to be right in front of it when a good set of waves came through would be hurled some distance up the tunnel. The second discovery lay on the newly visible seabed which was littered with golf balls, thousands of golf balls.

Ray turned the boat in towards the cliffs, easing the throttle back until the tinnie skimmed to a halt. The engine grumbled. Two-stroke fumes wafted across the boat. The swell rolled in towards us, lifted and lowered the tinnie and continued on towards the cliffs.

'You OK for this?' asked Ray.

'Yep.'

'Not afraid of sharks?'

'Certainly not.'

'Good. We brought you a pranger to try. Just don't hurt anyone, OK?'

Ray pointed to a long six-barbed handspear lying in the bottom of the boat. Few if any people would employ a handspear in competition. Sure, it has its uses and is potent in the right hands. But in spearing circles it is for social dives: it is what a parent might give a child on their first tentative snorkelling lesson.

Allan hurled the anchor over the side, letting the rope slide through his hands until he felt the anchor bite. Then Ray clicked the engine off.

When diving from small boats, the idea is to gear up and get in the water as soon as possible before the combination of tight wetsuit, outboard fumes and ocean swell makes you sick. I took a breath and rolled backwards over the side and into the cool relief of the sea. Two more splashes signalled that Ray and Allan had entered the water. They balanced their spearguns on their hips, the shafts pointing skyward, letting their riglines and buoys float out behind them, then they extended the rubbers back over the triggers. Spearguns loaded and pranger in hand we swam in towards the cliffs.

There is no set way to spear a fish. The gear, the technique employed, even the wetsuit worn by a diver working the reefs of Queensland's tropical north is very different to those of a diver spearfishing in the giant kelp beds and frigid seas off Tasmania's east coast. Add to that, spearfishing knowledge and skills are highly personalized. There are a few textbooks and in some instances older divers act as mentors to younger counterparts. But trial and error teach how to handle the cumbersome speargun. Practice and instinct tutor on stalking fish. And common sense will eventually dictate to even the most stubborn diver how deep they can dive and how far they can push themselves.

Over time, each diver learns for themselves how to read the sea from above and below the waves, how weather, tides, water temperature, even the phases of the moon, can attract some species and discourage others. They learn that fish are discerning creatures. In the words of marine biologist and world-ranked spearfisherman Dr Adam Smith, in order to catch a fish you must think like one. Smith holds that fish are invariably aware of the presence of the diver long before the diver sees them. Moreover, a fish may even recognize the threat posed by a speargun. The diver must always consider whether their shadow has alerted the fish to their presence; whether the fish's eyes are located to the front of the head (indicating that it has a blind spot if approached from behind); whether powerful attractions such as berley or lures will override warnings the fish receives from its other senses. Such knowledge comes with time in the water and practice, years of practice.

The sun climbed higher, sending shafts of sunlight plunging into the sea. It played like laser lights on rock ledges and boulders and brought colour to the kelp beds dancing in the ocean swell. Ray and Allan were about 30 metres apart: in the conditions, a comfortable distance for each to fish in peace, yet close enough for one to come to the other's aid if needed. They would take a breath, dive down and hang mid-water, then cruise over the massive sandstone slabs eroded from Malabar's cliff-line. Every so often they would stop and investigate a hole or crevice. Their movements appeared relaxed, effortless.

At one point I hung on the surface watching Ray 10 metres below. He was totally absorbed in what appeared to be a barren rock ledge. He didn't move. He just stared at the rock, his speargun aimed at a target that I could not see. There was a dull twang and Ray dragged a rock blackfish out from under the ledge. It twisted and turned in an effort to free itself from the spear. Ray scooped up the fish and headed to the surface. He threaded the rigline through the gills and out through the fish's mouth then killed the twitching animal with a knife to the brain. Not pretty, but death rarely is. His movements were quick and efficient, yet I saw none of the urgency I'd long associated with spearfishing competitions.

'You don't seem to take the comp too seriously', I said.

'No', he said. 'That's the good thing. If you just want to turn up, catch a few fish and go home, well, it's no big deal. That's enough for me these days.'

'Do you miss it?'

'Not a bit.'

He sounded positive but I couldn't help feeling his guard had just gone up. He looked over to see how Allan was progressing, reloaded his speargun and dived back down to wander on along the cliffs. Behind him the dead fish drifted down the rigline to the buoy. Allan and Ray had been mates for as long as I had known them. Their friendship originated years ago from a shared passion for spearfishing. Back then things were very different. They would hit the water like greyhounds hit the track, swimming out fast and hard, diving deep, covering as much ground as they could in an effort to hunt down their quarry before someone else beat them to it. No dive was out of bounds. If they had to swim an hour to reach the best fish they would get in the water and start swimming. If they had to hike 5 kilometres through scrub and then climb down a cliff face to get there, they'd strap their masks, fins and rigs to their backs and run.

Even social dives pushed boundaries. One time while Allan was working as bar manager on Hamilton Island in the Whitsundays, he and two friends borrowed a boat and headed out to the outermost reefs where the game boats hunted dolphin fish, sailfish and marlin. Out there, the reef falls away to open ocean in one sheer drop. The tides scream through and the ocean swell pounds the coral. There is little margin for error but for the bold lies the promise of mangrove jack, dogtooth tuna, Spanish mackerel and wahoo.

'Your kill has to be quick and clean, otherwise the sharks come in', Allan had told me over a game of pool one evening.

Six times the sharks came in, becoming bolder with each approach. Allan finally decided it was time to get back in the boat when a pack tore in from nowhere and ripped a 20 kilogram Spanish mackerel off his spear.

'It's weird with sharks. Sometimes you can dive with them and everything is fine. But you know just by looking at them if something is wrong. They hunch up and move erratically. You can almost hear the electricity in the water', he said.

Things changed in the summer of 1996. Allan had been out spearfishing with his brother Michael not far from where we were diving that morning. They entered the water together but went in different directions. It was only by chance that Michael found Allan lying unconscious on a rock ledge some 12 metres below.

'He thought it was just an old wetsuit on the bottom. Then he realized it was me', said Allan.

Three times Michael dived down for him. The first time he could not reach his unconscious brother. The second he swam down and attempted to drag Allan up from the bottom but did not have the strength. Allan sank back down to the ledge while Michael raced to the surface gasping for breath. On the third attempt Michael scrambled down and with everything he had, grabbed his brother and dragged him back up. As soon as he reached the surface Allan came around and found himself in his brother's arms.

The hospital diagnosis was shallow water or freediver blackout: 'the sudden loss of consciousness caused by oxygen starvation during the diver's ascent'. Allan had been stalking a fish, a good one, and pushed his limits just that bit too hard.

To his mates he was shaken but had survived to dive another day. I remember talking with Allan months after the incident. He recounted the dive and his near drowning, the realization of how important his family was to him and the guilt about what he had put them through. As he talked, a steady stream of tears rolled down his amiable face.

'I'd just got engaged to Peggy and nearly threw it all away. I still can't talk to her about it.'

Allan continued to roll up for the monthly spearfishing competition but the fire had left his belly. He would never push his dive limits again.

I watched him swim along the base of the cliffs and drop down under the water. After several rather clumsy attempts with the pranger I was quite content just to float around and take in the scenery so I swam over to his buoy and dived down, following the rigline. At its end I found Allan investigating a patch of kelp. He looked up, waved and pointed to the kelp. I had to return to the surface for air before I managed to see what was so intriguing. Allan followed shortly after, carrying a fish.

'Bit of butter, bit of garlic, some white wine', he said. Then he dispatched the quivering creature and threaded it onto his rigline.

We dived for around three hours before Ray and Allan decided they'd had enough and it was time to head back to Gunnamatta Bay. Between them they had speared four fish. In that time I'd managed to spear two rocks and a menacing piece of seaweed. At least I hadn't thrown up.

Merv Sheehan held court. He was seated at a table under the picnic shelter at the top of Gunnamatta Park. In front of him was a straggling line of competitors, their precious catches in sacks or plastic buckets at their feet, or dangling from lines slung over bare shoulders. One by one they stepped up and placed their fish on the scales hanging from a battered steel tripod set up next to Merv's table. At Merv's side sat a scribe in wetsuit long john, studiously calculating scores as the species and weight of each fish was announced.

The weigh-in is a well-worn ceremony, the time when spearfishing's pecking order is re-established, when the achievements of the day are displayed for all to see. The mood was more relaxed than at the beginning of the day. There was a barbecue under way. Wives stood chatting in small groups at the outer edge of proceedings while juniors slalomed through the crowd, clutching soft drinks, their mouths jammed with sausages and bread. The competitors laughed and joked but the eyes gave their true mood away, flitting from catch to catch, watching the scales, consciously and unconsciously judging themselves as each score was announced.

I stood off to one side with Ray and Allan. Their boat had been loaded back onto its trailer; their fish packed in ice for the trip home. It was time for a beer.

'Did you get what you wanted?' Ray asked, as he twisted the top off a stubbie and handed it to me.

'Enough to keep me going.' We sipped on our beers and conversation switched to fish, fast cars and things that go bang: did you know that a V8 Holden ute can travel at 180 kilometres an hour fully laden? Or that if a scuba tank exploded under a Volkswagen it could lift it 30 metres off the ground?

Allan smiled and nodded hello to a group of divers standing at the weigh-in scales. I knew them. Mark Colys, Lennie Goldsmith and Gunther Pfrengle — three men passionate about spearfishing, some might say to the point of obsession. Going by championship points they were, at that time, three of the best spearfishermen in New South Wales. They were good friends, but when it came to spearfishing each of them aimed to win. Nothing less.

All eyes were on Mark — a sinewy man in his thirties with intent brown eyes, his unruly hair stiff with salt. He still had his wetsuit on. It was old and worn, the legs cut away at the knees. He stood at the scales, a kingfish in his arms. At his feet was a large hessian sack holding the rest of his catch. One by one the fish were placed on the scales, Merv announcing the species and weight. Kingfish 7 kilos, mulloway 12.4 kilos, bonito 2.5 kilos — the list went on.

Ray Inkpen leaned back against the picnic shelter and sipped on his beer. I followed his gaze. Mark had moved aside. Sue Dockar now stood at the weigh-in scales, one of three of women taking part in the Alliman. She, too, still had her wetsuit on. Her speargun, rig and fish lay at her feet.

She was aged in her mid-forties. You would not describe her as big — just strong. Her honey-coloured hair was bedraggled from the sea, her hazel green eyes disguised by thick glasses. Sue was the person who Merv, upon first meeting, summed up as the most stubborn woman he had ever met and, over many years, came to regard as his closest, most loyal of friends.

SUE WHO?

Enjoyment has nothing to do with it.

Lennie Goldsmith

'What drives you, Sue?' It was a question first asked by a fourteen-year-old Mark Colys back in the early 1980s. In fact it was a question he considered regularly, as most Sunday mornings he was slumped over the side of Merv Sheehan's or Mick Shannessy's boat, vomiting into a cold rough sea while, in a boat somewhere close by, Sue Dockar would invariably be doing the same.

> I'd look at her sprawled over the back of the boat, then I'd look at myself and think, 'Why am I doing this? I'm sitting here spewing my guts up week after week, year in year out and getting nowhere'. Then I'd look at her and think, 'What keeps you going?'

It wasn't just Mark. Back then no one in the St George Spearfishing Club could quite work Sue out. She was female for a start. Now, they had nothing against females joining the club, it was just, well, they didn't tend to stick around for long — 'a couple of months and then it would all get too hard, the boat rides too rough, they'd get a boyfriend, break a nail and that would be it'.

By rights Sue should have thrown the towel in by now. She was sick every time she got in a boat and blind as a bat without her glasses, so the fact that she speared anything was a bloody miracle! But you had to hand it to her; she wouldn't give up. Come rain or shine Sue Dockar was there at the boat ramp waiting for the competition to begin. On that basis there was always space for Sue on someone's boat, always a smile and a nod when she weighed in her fish.

Mark stumbled into spearfishing in the late 1970s after he, his cousin Vlado Hric and friend Scottie Smiles were spotted snorkelling down and stealing crayfish from pots anchored off Shark Island south of Sydney. The fisherman who owned the pots was a member of the St George Spearfishing Club and a good friend of Merv's. He told him about the boys, swearing he'd give the little shits a hiding when he caught up with them. But Merv had other ideas.

'You want them to stop pinching your crays, then get them to join the club. When they start spearing they won't need to steal fish', he said.

The fisherman took the advice and, a few days later, approached the boys on one of Shark Island's surf-swept rock platforms. They used a burned matchstick to write Merv's telephone number on a piece of old cardboard. A week later, Mark, Vlado and Scottie were on his doorstep with ragged wetsuits and a duffle-bag full of scrounged dive gear.

Initially the boys dived from Merv's boat, under his guidance. Not that he needed to teach them much. They were fit, tenacious and bold and took to spearfishing with remarkable ease. All Merv had to do was impose a little discipline. Within a year, the boys were bringing in kingfish, jewfish and snapper. Within two they were on a par with some of the more competitive senior divers in the club. For all the boys, but especially Mark, what drove them was simple: they loved being out there, and they were there to be the best they could be. For Mark, in the end it didn't matter how much gut-wrenching, sweat-ridden nausea he had to put up with; he was determined to achieve his best.

For Sue Dockar things were very different. As far back as she could remember, she knew she wasn't 'the one'. In Sue's eyes that honour went to her sister. Sandra was her junior by thirteen months. She had long blonde hair, blue eyes and fair skin. Sue's hair was mousy, any sparkle in her eyes was obscured by her glasses and she sported a patchy tan.

'I was the geeky one. Tall and skinny and geeky', said Sue.

Back then the family lived in a rambling old two-storey house in Sydney's Summer Hill. At the time Sue couldn't quite understand why her parents didn't get along and it was never openly discussed. All she knew was that they fought, that she, her sister and mother slept upstairs and their father's room was downstairs. That was just the way it was and the way it stayed for years.

She had a great affection for her father. He was a quiet, practical man and when something needed fixing he would walk out to the shed, select a few tools and attend to the task. As a child Sue would follow a few steps behind with her own tiny tool set, her own tiny drill and hammer and together they would patiently repair leaking pipes, nail back wayward fence palings, silence squeaking doors and rebuild ancient lawnmowers. And on the rare occasions when there was nothing to fix she would construct her own little world, alone in the backyard.

> We had a huge persimmon tree and it used to drop fruit all the time. My father had a workbench sort of thing under there and I used to go and hide in it. It had doors and all these exciting things.

'I used to use it as my cubby house and climb the tree', she said.

As she grew older all Sue really wanted was to fit in, to be liked. But in the harsh world of adolescence, geeks rarely make it to the upper echelons of popularity and what attention there is invariably involves shame and ridicule. So Sue learned to fade into the background both at home and at school, to keep her feelings to herself and to cherish friendship.

She was neither ambitious nor academically brilliant but she was good at sport. So she directed her energy and passion into basketball and table tennis, and when home life got too much she would wander down to Ashfield municipal pool and swim her frustrations away. But the sense of belonging she yearned for never came. Once the games were over, adolescent rules came into force once more. To Sue, it seemed as though she was destined to live as a fringe dweller.

Her parents separated when she was sixteen. She recalls it as a cold but mercifully clean break. Her mother rented a small unit on the other side of the railway station to their family home. A few days later she moved out.

Mum said, 'Are you going to come? It will help with the rent'. My sister wanted to but I didn't. We had a big old house and I was fine there and I had a job nearby. But Mum was doing it tough so I had to go.

Sue hated the flat. She hated the poky, airless rooms, the sounds and smells of other people. But most of all she hated being away from her father. So she saved up her money, bought a bike and most evenings would cycle 'home'.

Dad and I, we'd just sit there and watch TV together. We liked murder mysteries, sport, nature and adventure docos, and travel — travel anywhere. I loved reading too. I had heaps of books there. I had three encyclopaedias in the bookcase. I used to flick through them all the time. The first time I ever saw the Great Barrier Reef it was in one of those books.

Mum didn't say anything about me seeing Dad. She knew I didn't like being in the flat. Whenever she could she'd take me and Sandra away down the coast to visit friends. I suppose that's how it all really started for me. One time we were down near Jervis Bay and someone lent me a mask and snorkel. It was just a normal dive mask, not prescription lenses or anything, but it gave a fair bit of magnification under the water. I was eighteen and I remember wading out from the boat ramp and putting my head under the water and thinking, 'Wow, this is incredible!' The water was shallow and clear and everywhere I looked there were little fish and tiny crabs and when I swam further around the rocks I found anemones and kelp and different coloured algae growing.

It was the most amazing experience. At the time, all I wanted was to escape from my life. When I put that mask on, just being able to dive down under the water and swim with the fish, I felt a sense of freedom I'd never felt before.

From that point on Sue dived whenever and wherever she could. While other teenage girls were content to sit on Sydney beaches, she would spend hours snorkelling around the reefs and rocky outcrops, and on her trips away with her mother she would set off alone to explore the headlands and bays along the NSW south coast. When a family friend offered to take her diving with St George Spearfishing Club she leapt at the offer.

Initially it wasn't the competition that attracted me. All I saw was an opportunity to get out on the ocean and try something new. I loved it, but it was hard going. I was sick as soon as the boat anchored up and I didn't have prescription lenses fitted in my mask at first, so I didn't have that sharp vision you need for spearfishing.

Merv was one of the first people I met when I joined the club and he gave me a lot of advice and encouragement but I can't say anyone took me aside and taught me how to spear. You've got to remember that was the 1970s and back then when you hit the water you were pretty much on your own. At first I tried to see what the guys were doing but most of the time they would just take off and I wasn't real happy about following anyone. All I could do was get out there as much as I could and push myself every time.

Sue dived with the club for a year. Then, when she was twenty-one, she left Australia and spent the next six years travelling and working her way around the world. In late March of 1980 she was working as a nanny in Montreal.

A letter arrived from Dad. He said he had been diagnosed with cancer of the throat. I had a bit of money saved but it took a while for me to get enough for a flight home. By that stage the cancer had spread. Dad died in April. I got back in May.

While Sue was away her father had moved to a unit in Sydney's outer west. All Sue remembers is the shabby appearance of the building, the constant noise of traffic and his tiny dismal rooms crammed with belongings from the old house.

I went into the bedroom. I found my old encyclopaedias and his Western Suburbs Leagues medallion and I thought of how we used to sit and watch TV. I started stripping the bed. It was the big four-poster bed from our old house and it just about filled the room. Under the pillow I found a knife. I remember sitting down on the bed turning the knife around in my hands. All I could think of was him lying there dying in that horrible flat and being so frightened that he slept with a knife.

She left with four possessions: the old family car, her encyclopaedias, her father's medallion and his knife. Everything else was sold.

A few days later she phoned Merv. For a while they talked family matters, then gradually conversation moved to what had been happening with the club, who was in whose boat and when the next dive was scheduled. On the first Sunday in June, Sue was back at Gunnamatta Bay boat ramp. Old friends smiled and hugged her. At the age of twenty-seven, for the first time in her life, she felt she was where she belonged.

Just a fortnight after she cleaned out her father's flat, she met Greg Dockar. She was staying at her uncle's home in San Souci. There was a tennis club close by and a friend persuaded her to sign up for the Wednesday evening competition. The first match she played, Greg was on the opposite side of the net. Over a series of dates, she found they shared the same love of sport and outdoor pursuits, the same quiet dependable nature. But most of all they had a great affection for one another.

Six months later Greg proposed. They bought a block of land in the outer Sydney suburb of Menai and by November 1981 they were married. They slept on a mattress in their half-built house and cooked their meals over a gas burner set up on the garage slab. During the week Greg worked as an instruments technician at AWA; Sue worked as a secretary at Port Botany. On Saturdays they worked on the house. On Sundays, Sue would pack her guns into the back of the car and they would head to the coast.

Greg never took to spearfishing. As far as he was concerned, there were much easier ways of landing a fish on a plate. Some Sunday mornings he would head across to Kurnell, or down through the Royal National Park to Garie, Marley or Wattamolla beaches and fish off the rocks. Other times he would jump in the boat with Sue and while she dived he would hang a line over the side of the boat.

At first, Greg's backseat role had a few of the spearos scratching their heads. But it was obvious that his love for Sue was genuine and, by now, Sue was one of them. So after a while the questions waned. Sue dived and Greg Dockar melted into the spearfishing crowd like everyone else.

COMPETING

In the last twenty-five years four divers have won the Australian nationals seventeen times. These are the guys who you really want to test yourself against. These are the guys you want to beat.

Ian Puckeridge, six times Australian spearfishing champion, world ranked spearfisherman

As one might expect, spearfishing competitions have a strict hierarchy. At the bottom are the boat-based club and interclub (zone) events which each run once a month. While these events attract a core of highly competitive divers, they are fairly relaxed. Things get a little more intense at the two- to three-day state championships. These are usually land-based events or 'rock hops', meaning competition starts from a designated point and competitors run and swim out to their dive sites, and a few hours later, swim and run all the way back. They must also carry all their gear, namely mask, snorkel and fins, a weight belt weighing between 4 and 12 kilograms, speargun, rigline, float, dive knife, catch bag and spare mask straps, and their catch, which could weigh anywhere between 6 and 20 kilos. Any assistance means instant disqualification.

The year culminates with the national spearfishing championships. Like the state championships, the event is run over two to three days, with each day's competition taking five to six hours. Again, as in the state championships, competitors start and finish at a designated point and have to carry all their gear and catch unaided.

Typically, competition at this level involves a 7 kilometre run and/or a 6 kilometre swim, often in rough seas, deep water and strong currents. Climate, water temperature and fear of sharks add a psychological dimension to the event that few other sports would tolerate. In Tasmania and South Australia, for instance, the summer air temperature can reach 40°C while the sea temperature remains around 13°C. Great white sharks cruise near shore reefs and rocky outcrops. The mind can play some very interesting games in those conditions.

The 1983 Australian Underwater Championships were to be run out of Gladstone, on the central Queensland coast. It is a small town, originally built around a meat works and a small fishing industry. More recent times have seen it dominated by an aluminium smelter and the largest container port in the southern hemisphere. Pretty it is not. But it is the port from which fishing and charter vessels make their way out to the Capricorn and Bunker groups of islands at the southern reaches of the Great Barrier Reef.

In winter on these islands you can sit under the trees and watch whales breach less than 100 metres away. On summer nights, loggerhead turtles haul themselves ashore to lay their eggs. In the cool light of dawn you can walk out from these deserted islands and dive with manta rays, dolphins and a mind-boggling array of tropical fish.

Not surprisingly, the venue attracted strong interest, with some seventy-five divers signing up for the championships. Some were willing to travel thousands of kilometres on dirt roads and across deserts just to take part. There was no big prize money at stake. What was up for grabs was the knowledge of who was the best spearo in Australia and where they, personally, rated on that scale.

For Sue Dockar the national championships seemed like a natural progression — another milestone in the life of a woman growing increasingly certain of who she was and what she wanted out of life. She was well and truly over her sea sickness. She also had prescription lenses fitted in her dive mask. Suddenly, there was new shape and clarity to kelp beds, reefs and rock ledges. 'After that, spearfishing became a whole lot more fun', she said.

> I started bringing in good fish — flathead, flounder, bream, Tasmanian trumpeter. Not jaw-dropping catches by any means but it was enough to boost my monthly scores. It also kept me and Greg fed for most of the year — we didn't have much money so everything I caught went into the freezer. It still does.

From Merv's perspective it was straightforward enough. Sometime in the previous year the woman who couldn't see without her glasses, who was sick every time she got in a boat, had become highly competitive. He still remembers the day she weighed in her first snapper: 4.5 kilograms. A few weeks later she placed a large kingfish on the scales — clean killed with a spear to the brain. That turned a few heads! But for Merv the clincher came at the 1982 state championships where Sue not only beat some of Merv's junior protégés, she beat a fair few men. He asked if she would compete in the 1983 national championships in Gladstone. 'You're more than capable, and you've certainly got enough points to be in the team', he told her.

Sue smiled, as she always did, and told him she'd have to discuss it with Greg.

So it was that in late December 1982, the Dockars headed north up the New England Highway, the rear of their Subaru station wagon crammed with dive gear, clothes, food, pillows and toilet rolls. By the time they reached the Queensland border after ten hours on the road the original excitement of escaping from Sydney had mellowed into the tedium of a marathon drive as bush, paddocks, homesteads flashed past.

For Sue it would be her first national championships, her first time diving on the Great Barrier Reef. The prospect filled her with anticipation and excitement but also a slight nervousness. For a moment ghosts of her childhood played on her mind. Then, without really thinking, she shut them away and returned to the present. She vowed her team mates would never see that side of her. All they would see was the woman they knew: calm, quiet Sue Dockar, the woman who would give the competition everything she had.

Mark, Vlado and Scottie had also signed up. It had taken a fair bit to persuade their parents to let them go, particularly in Mark's case. Despite his obvious skills, they were uncomfortable with his diving, sharing every parent's nightmare that one day they'd wave off their oldest son and he would never return. But Mark persisted, gently wearing them down with reassurances. 'It will be OK, Mum, the older guys are looking out for us juniors.' 'Come on, Dad, it's not like off Sydney. They water is warm up there and you can see for miles. It is safe, easy diving.' 'I promise you, Dad, I won't do anything stupid.'

It was only when veteran spearfisherman Keith Brabham offered to drive the boys up to Gladstone that Mark's father relented. High on a cocktail of relief and excitement Mark ran the few streets from his San Souci home to Vlado's house. 'Dad said I can go!' he blurted out as Vlado pulled back the flyscreen door. 'I can go to Gladstone.'

Two months later, Mark, Vlado and Scottie were sitting in Keith's old Holden en route to Gladstone, Queensland and the Great Barrier Reef. It was their first trip away without their families — their first big adventure.

Keith Brabham, otherwise known as the Blabster, was a seasoned abalone diver and spearo. He was an amiable bloke, tall and slim with cropped red hair, sharp eyes and a thick moustache that drooped across his lips. His adolescent charges knew that stored up in his mind were years of experience, the type of knowledge that meant the difference between winning a competition and being no one. For the next couple of days the four of them were in a car together heading north. Not being ones to let an opportunity go by, the angel-faced boys began to pump old Blabster for all the information they could get.

His stories blended one into the next, egged on by the constant questions of the younger men. He told them tales of his navy days, of abalone diving off Tasmania and Victoria, of breaching whales and playful seals and silent sharks that circle lone divers many kilometres from shore. But it was the reef they wanted to know about and the conversation was purposefully steered northward.

'You've got to understand it's different up there', said Blabster, finally bowing to the pressure.

> Everything revolves around the currents. Before you even think of getting in the water you've got to know the tide times, where the island is and how the currents meet the island. That will tell you where the fish are.

He told them about the different species of fish — how some only came onto the bomboras at high tide and others appeared at low tide. How the large pelagic fish, the Spanish mackerels and barracudas, sit on the edge of the current like warships waiting for battle to commence. He told them it was more than just knowing your fish, they had to know the cues — like the seabirds congregating where currents meet, like baitfish moving fast, or the silver glint off in the distance that may be the only warning of an approaching tuna.

Listening is a skill the old often claim is lacking in the young. But his audience sat in silence as Blabster talked. And when his stories waned they asked more questions, soaking up the information and salting it away for future reference.

'What about the sharks?' asked Mark.

'You want the sharks to leave you alone, then you kill your fish properly', he instructed them.

You don't just spear them, you cut their throat and snap back their neck so that they're not flapping around on your float. Make sure you do it. Make sure you kill every single fish.

It was late afternoon. Neon lights flickered into life on the edge of yet another small town. Conversation turned to whether they should drive on or pull in somewhere for the night. Blabster said he was tired and suggested stopping. The boys wanted to keep going, but Blabster was calling the shots.

Mark leaned back on the seat and shut his eyes. In his mind he was already in Queensland, looking out over the flat turquoise water, making out the vague shapes of the coral heads below. He tried to imagine what it would be like to dive down and still be able to see forever. He could see the multi-coloured fish of Blabster's stories. Feel the trigger of the gun resting against his fingers. Hear the dull twang of the rubbers as they sent the spear hurtling towards the fish.

GEARING UP

I saw Ray down at Narooma a few years back.
He came up and said, 'I'm Ray Inkpen'. He seemed unsure
as to whether he should talk to me. I think he thought
I was going to thump him. I went over and told him,
'It wasn't your fault'.

Greg Dockar

In 1974, Dan Meyer devised a matrix to help with analysing mountaineering accidents. The matrix was subsequently refined by Jed Williamson and went on to become one of the best known, most frequently cited analysis tools in disaster management. The matrix sets out three basic causes of accidents, namely unsafe conditions, unsafe acts and errors of judgment. In some instances, only one factor — a lightning strike, say — may cause an accident. More commonly, accidents occur when a number of factors come together, either gradually increasing until they overwhelm the safety system, or lining up like dominos, waiting for that one gentle flick to send them on a catastrophic course.

This matrix can just as easily be applied to the events off Gladstone in early January 1983. No one intended events to unfold the way they did. In hindsight, the divers interviewed felt the 1983 spearfishing championships should never have been held. Not on that day, not at that island, not in those conditions. But hindsight is a wonderful thing. Everyone becomes an expert, offering sage advice based on cold, hard fact, skilfully ignoring the subtle forces that drove, bullied and cajoled even the smartest divers to disregard their instincts.

At the centre of proceedings was Ray Inkpen, then a twenty-two-year-old Royal Australian Air Force technician. There was a picture of him in Gladstone's *Morning Bulletin* on 6 January 1983. It was taken on the lawn of Gladstone District Hospital the day Sue Dockar was found. It shows him as a fit and muscular young man. He is looking across at a relieved Merv Sheehan, who is holding up a jubilant Greg Dockar. But Ray looks sad and beat.

Ray Inkpen had moved to Queensland from Western Australia eighteen months before the Gladstone championships. At that stage there were two passions in his life — the RAAF and spearfishing. If Ray wasn't working, he'd be diving. If it was too rough to dive he'd be ensconced in one of the workshops on the Ipswich airbase where he was stationed, repairing his spearguns, or stripping down the outboard from his tinnie, or helping a friend from the Underwater Adventurers Club repair their gear. There was always something to do in preparation for the next dive.

Every second weekend Ray would rise before dawn, hitch his tender and head off for a coastal rendezvous with the club. There was good diving within an hour's drive north or south of the airbase, but more often than not the men launched their boats at Redcliffe boat ramp, the set-off point for Moreton and Stradbroke Islands, about 30 kilometres off the south Queensland coast.

Even on the best of days, in a fast, seaworthy powerboat, wind chop, sandbars and a cat's cradle of currents made the hour-long journey across Moreton Bay a hair-raising, spine-jarring experience. But the image that stayed in Ray's mind was of their boats screaming across the bay in the early morning light, and the deep, clean water on the seaward sides of the islands. In the mornings they freedived for crayfish; after lunch they dived for coral trout, tuskfish and cobia. At night they would set up a beach camp on Moreton Island and boil up cheap red cask wine, brandy and fruit in an old pot to make gluhwein.

'We'd drink the juice and eat the fruit', says Ray, and he smiles the smile of good memories. 'It was a good life.'

Six months after his move to Queensland, Ray signed up as secretary of the state branch of the Australian Underwater Federation, the organizers of the 1983 Australian Underwater Championships in Gladstone. He handled much of the paperwork for the organizing committee. He took the minutes, wrote the cheques, banked competition fees and generally helped out where he could.

To all but the participants, the event schedule seemed a little bizarre. It featured finswimming, where swimmers propelled by a massive semicircular monofin 'dolphin' kick their way over 25 to 800 metre distances; underwater hockey, a game invented by the British navy where two teams of six divers battle over a plastic-coated ice hockey puck on the bottom of a swimming pool; film fishing, where breathhold and scuba divers photograph, rather than catch, as many fish as they can; a scuba diving theory and practical test; and, of course, spearfishing.

At that stage Ray Inkpen had his sights set on being part of the Queensland spearfishing team. He booked leave from work well in advance, dived every competition, pushed his depths and breathholds, studied textbooks on the reefs, fish species and currents before he went to bed at night. Then he got the telephone call.

It was Ray Oakey. At that point, he was the convener of the Gladstone championship. Ray was a fireman and the bushfire season was kicking off. Anyway, he told me he was pulling out. To be honest, with the shifts he worked and the things he saw I don't know how he kept going with the organizing committee as long as he did. With him gone, basically there was no one else to do the job so I took it on. Of course that meant I couldn't compete.

By the time Ray took the reins, the Brisbane-based organizing committee had booked Gladstone Memorial Pool for the finswimming and underwater hockey events, made reservations at the Tanyalla Conference Centre in the nearby town of Boyne-Tannum to accommodate around 200 competitors, officials and family who were expected to attend the championship, and chartered the vessel *Reefseeker* to take competitors out to Erskine and Masthead Islands for the spear and film fishing events. There was only one problem: the dates scheduled for the spear and film fishing coincided with some of the strongest tides of the year. They were less than ideal conditions for putting seventy or so divers in the water.

The organizing committee considered shifting the competition to later in the week when the currents were not so strong. That would mean swapping the event with underwater hockey or finswimming. But Gladstone Memorial Pool was only available between the eighth and the fourteenth of January — the booking could not be changed. Then they considered moving the event to a venue not exposed to the tides. But the alternative sites were much further offshore and the cost of chartering a vessel would increase dramatically. They considered holding the spearfishing competition the following week. But that would wreak havoc with annual leave and accommodation arrangements. In the end, they decided to stick with their original plan and hope things would work out.

On 31 December 1982 Ray Inkpen was seated behind an old desk in the makeshift office he had set up at Tanyella Convention Centre. A portable fan turned gently in the corner of the room, stirring the humid air, occasionally lifting the edges of the neatly piled forms, brochures and maps he had carefully laid out on the desk in front of him. It was early morning, but already the room was heavy with the dense tropical heat synonymous with Queensland's cyclone season. Ray's Australian Underwater Federation T-shirt and standard issue stubbies were tainted with sweat and he had kicked off his well-worn thongs to let his bare feet draw in the cool of the linoleum floor.

There were two days to go before the spearfishing kicked off and, from Ray's perspective at least, things were humming along. There were the odd grumbles about the itinerary, but there was always someone who felt they could have arranged things better. As for accommodation, most people had settled in, although a few were somewhat disappointed to find they were 25 kilometres outside of Gladstone, in a town where sandflies were the most prolific local fauna.

Ray had spent the previous two weeks camped with some of the Queensland team at North West Island, not far from where the spearfishing competition would take place. Each morning they would fire up the boats and head out to dive the massive reef which encircled the island. At night they cooked fish on a camp fire, knocked back a beer or two and told the stories that spearos like to tell: of the huge fish they'd nearly caught, the sharks they'd seen and the boats they dreamed of buying if they ever won the lottery.

Now it was down to business. On the morning of 31 December 1982 Ray's mind was filled with figures, times and schedules. That's probably why he didn't pay too much attention when a young couple quietly entered the office.

'Sue and Greg Dockar', said Ray, scanning down a column of names and pointing out through the door of the office. 'Yep, you're up there on the left.'

In the early 1980s, Boyne-Tannum was a working man's town straddling the mangrove-lined banks of the Boyne River. On the northern side of the river lay Boyne Island and the largest alumina smelter in the southern hemisphere. On the southern side was Tannum Sands, so named because tannin from the surrounding eucalypts and scrub had turned the sands a deep caramel colour. In fact the soft brown sands run from the northern tip of Boyne Island down to Wild Cattle Island south of Tannum Sands. It is a shallow stretch of coast and at low tide out-of-towners can be lulled into thinking it is one long, wide beach. Then the tide creeps back in and within no time at all the sandflats and creek beds disappear under sediment-laden waves.

For many years, life for the residents of Boyne-Tannum was dominated by the tides. Even a trip to the pub was dictated by the times of high and low water. At low tide the people from Boyne Island used to walk across the river's mangroves and mudflats to Tannum Sands and up to the hotel at the top of the hill. At high tide it was a 30 kilometre trip out of Boyne Island, onto the Bruce Highway and then up to the pub via the old Tannum Road. The local kids knew an opportunity when they saw it and charged a dollar a pop to row pub patrons across the Boyne River. That budding industry died when the bridge was built in 1980 and the communities of Boyne Island and Tannum Sands became one.

Tanyella sits on the Tannum Sands side of the bridge. It was built in 1979 by the Anglican Church. Apart from the odd coat of paint, its barrack-style accommodation has changed little over the past twenty-five years. The dormitory style rooms still stand, ten to a block, a flyscreen door guarding the entrance to each room. There is a large communal kitchen and dining room at one end of the centre, shower facilities and laundry at the other. The sandflies are everywhere.

Sue still has a few photographs of Tanyella. One shows a long, single-storey white fibro building backing onto bare dirt, eucalypts and scrub. In the tradition of Queensland dwellings, the block is raised off the ground on stilts with a corrugated tin roof and a wide verandah running its full length. Men stripped down to shorts or speedos are sprawled along the verandah's wooden boards. They clutch bottles of beer and look content to wallow in the heat and conversations about nothing much.

Sue and Greg picked their way across that crowded verandah to their room. Inside, they found two single metal-framed beds, a chair, a desk, a ceiling fan and a louvered window looking out onto bush. It was basic but clean and, being a couple, at least they had a room to themselves. Anyway, after eighteen hours straight on the road, Sue was content to turn on the ceiling fan and fall back onto one of the beds with Greg.

It was New Year's Eve and less than forty-eight hours to the national spearfishing championship. Tanyella was starting to buzz. Sue could hear it in the excited conversations that wafted past their room and the rapid footsteps of juniors as they thundered back and forth across the verandahs.

> We could have walked out of our room and spent the rest of the day on the verandah with the Queensland team, trying to find out more about the dive venue and the best strategies to spearfish on the reef. But that's never been my way.

'I just wanted to rest up and collect my thoughts', she said.

For a while they lay in each other's arms, content to let the party go on around them. Yes, she had to catch up with her team mates. And sometime that day they had to head into Gladstone to pick up the skivvy and blockout that Merv Sheehan had insisted all NSW team members acquire for the competition. 'Cover up or that sun will burn you to a crisp', he'd said. Sue wasn't game to face Merv without first buying that skivvy. But for the moment it could wait.

By the time Sue and Greg surfaced from their room their friends had moved on, so they wandered around Tanyella for a while and then followed one of the dirt tracks down to the beach. The tide was still high and only a slim ribbon of sand separated the sea from the scrub. Off to the north lay the gentle green hills of Facing Island. To the south was a long steady arc of sea, sand and wispy she-oaks permanently bent northward in testament to the prevailing winds.

Sue and Greg spent the rest of the morning bodysurfing in the small waves and sunbaking on the hot brown sand. Greg remembers sitting on the beach with his arms wrapped around Sue.

He remembers pulling her close to him and kissing the back of her neck. 'It was one of those days when everything felt right with the world', said Greg.

I had Sue, we were together in Queensland and in two days we would be out on the Great Barrier Reef. I thought we were so lucky. I thought, 'Life doesn't get much better than this'.

Within twelve hours of their arrival, Mark Colys, Vlado Hric and Scottie Smiles had made quite an impression on Tannum Sands. First, there was the cane toad incident. Blabster and the boys had arrived at Tanyella right on dusk. After a long day's driving, Blabster had fallen onto one of the bunks and gone to sleep. Mark, Vlado and Scottie were left to their own devices just as the first of the fat ugly toads hopped and crawled out of hiding onto Tanyella's lawns and paths. The boys had never seen cane toads before. At first they stood and stared at the bloated grey blobs. Then they poked them with sticks to see what they would do. Then Scottie decided to investigate further.

'We warned him not to, but Scottie just had to pick one up', said Vlado. 'Next thing you know this toad arches its back and squirts poison all over him.'

Scottie screamed, dropped the toad and ran off to the showers clutching his face. It was a good half hour before he came out again, a line of welts marking the passage of the poison on his skin.

With one of their number wounded, the boys retrieved a palm frond from the undergrowth. They stripped away the leaves, revealing a long, heavy branch with a mean-looking stump. Then they decided to see how far a toad could travel with their improvised four iron up its backside. Their first attempts concluded with loud splats and bits of toad flying in all directions. Then they tried addressing the toads slightly lower down. This technique propelled more than a dozen toads onto roofs and gutters and several more clean over the accommodation blocks.

It wasn't long before someone was hit by a flying toad and the boys were ordered to hand over the branch. It was getting dark and they were told to get some rest. But Mark, Vlado and Scottie had other ideas. By that stage they had teamed up with another NSW junior, Lennie Goldsmith.

'The first time I saw Lennie was in a weigh-in ring back in Sydney', said Mark.

> Someone pointed him out to us. He said, 'You see that big red-headed fella down there, he's the state junior champion'. Lennie was a pretty big jerker in comparison to me and Vlado. We still hadn't filled out and were pretty scrawny.

Now the short and the tall were partners in crime. Lennie had spotted a sizeable mango tree in the backyard of a neighbouring property. The boys' mission was to retrieve enough mangoes to feed the camp for the next three days. They launched their sortie under the cover of darkness, clambering up the awning of an adjacent shop and shinning their way up the tree. No one can remember exactly how many hessian sackloads of fruit they hauled back to their room, or how many mangoes the boys gorged themselves on that night. But Blabster can remember the morning after: four boys with gut ache, one of them with a large welt down the side of his face, and dead cane toads everywhere.

Holding the reins on four teenage boys was no easy task, particularly when they were a long way from home and running on pure adrenaline. The best Blabster could do was try and direct their energy back into spearfishing and the forthcoming championship. He told them to clean up the toads, then sat them down on the verandah outside their room with their guns, rigs and floats strewn around them. He told them to check every piece of their gear.

> Check your rigline. Make sure it is sound and easy to tie. That way if you get caught in a current you can tie yourself off on the coral and rest. Make sure your line is the right length for the depth of water. There is no point carrying 30 metres of line in 10 metres of water. Twenty metres is ample. Check the prangers are straight and sharp, replace split or worn rubbers.

'Check it now and make sure its right because it's too late to do it when you're out on the reef', he told them.

Blabster was a keen roll-your-own man, Camel being his tobacco of choice. The boys had taken turns rolling his cigarettes as they progressed up the eastern Australian seaboard. By the time they reached Tannum Sands, Vlado could roll a cigarette with one hand. When they had finished prepping their gear, they once again took turns rolling cigarettes while Blabster told them about his time diving the reef for highly prized coral trout.

He told them that the coral trout had turreted eyes, which meant the fish could take a wide scan of the world without moving.

'And they are the fastest thing on the planet', he said.

> I've watched them sitting under a piece of coral and then exploding three to four times their own body length after a fish. So you watch and wait for it to look away before you pull that trigger, or all you'll spear is coral.

Vlado, Mark and Scottie might have been a touch on the wild side, but Blabster saw three top divers in the making. While they were in his care he tried to instil the fundamentals of spearfishing on the reef: go quietly; let the fish come to you; kill every fish you catch;

read the currents; and if you get caught out, use your rigline to tie off on the coral. That basic knowledge combined with their raw energy should see them through their first national spearfishing title. He told them these things time and time again.

He never thought for a minute it might save their lives.

CURRENTS

I came past the island a few months back. Right on sunset, it was. I had a bunch of young blokes in the boat with me and I told them what happened. Just telling them sent a chill down my spine.

Gunther Pfrengle

Erskine Island lies 65 kilometres off Gladstone. It is small — barely 2 hectares of land enclosing a shallow lagoon. The lagoon is skirted by a fringing reef that drops away to sand at around 20 metres. Like many of its neighbours in the Capricorn and Bunker groups of islands, Erskine Island is a coral cay: a thin strip of land formed over thousands of years from the materials of the reef beneath it, the seeds of its hardy vegetation carried by the wind and the tides, and discarded in the droppings of sea birds. Apart from the torrential downpours of the cyclone season, there is no fresh water. There are no gullies or hillsides to shelter in when storms rage or the sun beats down. It is little more than a speck of crushed coral sand, scrub and stunted trees, almost lost in the vast turquoise seascape of the Coral Sea.

The closest encounter most people have with Erskine Island is a fleeting glance from air-conditioned tour boats en route to Heron

Island dive resort. By the time those passengers reach their luxurious accommodation most will have forgotten Erskine Island existed. For those who attended the 1983 spearfishing competition, however, that tiny speck of land still represents the ultimate test of a diver's endurance.

The problem was not so much the island but the tides. All seas and oceans are subject to tides: periodic rises and falls in water level associated with the gravitational forces that maintain the sun, moon and earth in their orbits. The largest and most intense movements, known as spring tides, occur when the gravitational forces of the sun and moon act together. The smallest range of movements, known as neap tides, occurs when the moon is in the first and last quarters.

The tidal range, the difference between the height of the high water and the next succeeding low water, varies from place to place as well as with the phases of the moon. Along much of the Queensland coast the tidal range is roughly 3 metres at spring tide and half a metre at neap tide. But in some areas the tidal range can be as much as 10 metres.

Rather than rising and falling as one body of water, tidal movements appear to radiate from a particular point. For the Great Barrier Reef that point is somewhere deep in the Coral Sea. On the incoming tide, water is drawn from the open ocean over the continental shelf, through the shallow labyrinth of reefs, bomboras and channels to the mainland. On the outgoing tide it races back. In each instance these geographic features act in the same way a spillway acts on water from a dam, concentrating and directing its flow and culminating in the notorious currents that rip, eddy and surge their way across the Great Barrier Reef.

The moon was full on 30 December 1982 and some of the highest high tides of the year were predicted for the following three days. The first heat of the spearfishing competition was scheduled for 2 January 1983 — the third day. Gladstone tidal predictions indicated a low tide of 0.62 metres at 5.01 am, followed by a 4.67

metre high tide at 11.37am. Erskine Island would provide little, if any, protection for those taking part. Even the fittest diver familiar with reef currents would be hard pressed to make headway in such a movement of water. Spearfishermen from Yeppoon down to Bundaberg called for the event to be rescheduled. Ironically, the most vocal protests came from the man favoured to win the competition, whatever the conditions on the day. His name was Ralph Whalley.

Legend had it that Ralph could out-dive, out-spear, out-fight and out-drink the rest of the world and the French. While lesser men mowed their lawns and washed their cars, Ralph would disappear for days, even weeks, off diving, fishing or stirring up the patrons of some outback pub. Ralph Whalley, by all accounts, was the real man's hero.

That was the legend. The man I met stood over 183 centimetres tall. He had a barrel chest, a deep tan and forearms like Christmas hams, thanks to decades of working on fishing boats. He had a kind face and despite his years and greying hair, every so often he'd flash a grin that made him look like a teenage boy caught in the midst of mischief.

Ralph and his wife Anne hail from Bundaberg, a midcoast Queensland town best known for its potent dark rum. An art deco post office graces the town centre's wide, palm-lined streets and an old rail line still runs through the main shopping precinct, taking cage load upon cage load of burned sugar cane from the fields to the refinery.

They lived then, and still do now, in a cottage on the eastern side of town. Around the back of their home is a large aluminium shed where an assortment of metal- and wood-working tools hang on the walls and fishing nets are stowed on reels a metre across. On hot summer days, Ralph's pig-hunting dogs sleep in the shed, lounging contentedly across his work bench and over the cool steel of the barbecue plate. Sometimes when his friends are in trouble or down on their luck they sleep out there too.

Ralph has been spearfishing since he was eight years old and working fishing boats since he was thirteen. He doesn't know what his lung capacity is or how deep he can dive. Nor does he really care. If there's a fish to be caught or a net is snagged he just thinks his heart rate down, jumps off the back of his boat and drops to the bottom. No big deal.

In 1982 Ralph was thirty-two years old. Back then he was regularly freediving to 30 metres and beyond, sometimes at night, much of the time off the stern of his prawn trawler many kilometres offshore. Quite how he did it baffled those around him. A decade earlier one of his lungs collapsed as the result of an abscess — something he blames on a brief stint working as a diver clearing the cutter head of the Burnett River dredge. The lung reinflated but was significantly scarred and for a while he was coughing up blood. On top of that, smoking, drinking and partying hard were as much a part of Ralph's life as diving and fish. In fact, he long ago gained notoriety for downing a bottle of Stone's Green Ginger Wine on the journey to the dive site and smoking a cigarette just before he entered the water. Ralph remains adamant that Stone's Green Ginger Wine followed by a good heave over the side of the boat is the best cure for a hangover. It is a source both of great irritation and fascination that Ralph Whalley, after a night on the town, a bottle of Stone's and a cigarette can still dive deeper on his one good lung and catch better fish than the swag of health-conscious young turks left in his wake.

Despite the wild antics, those who know Ralph regard the man and what he says with respect. 'He's switched on to the sea in a way that few people are', is how one puts it. 'There's not much Ralph doesn't know about the reef.'

In 1982 Ralph had one Australian spearfishing title under his belt and was the favourite to win the men's title at the 1983 championships off Gladstone. Why? Because his main rival, Yeppoon diver, David Stubberfield, had boycotted the competition on account of the currents. And while there were still plenty of good spearos hot on Ralph's tail, the trump card in spearfishing is local knowledge. Everyone knew the Capricorn and Bunker Groups were where Ralph worked, where he played, where he would disappear to when dry land was a hard place to be.

Even so, Ralph was unhappy with the competition from the word go. Twenty years later he sketched out his reasons for me on a chart. The chart mapped the waters from Sandy Cape in the south up to the Keppel Isles in the north. The Capricorn and Bunker groups of islands were enclosed within a perimeter of neat dashes which formed the shape of a gun. Erskine Island sat on the grip, an insignificant blue smudge midway between Masthead Island to the west and Wistari Reef to the east.

There was a long pause as Ralph drew the movements of the water around Erskine Island, nearby Masthead Island and Wistari Reef. Bold red lines represented the powerful and uncompromising currents that had been predicted for 2 January 1983. The lines flanked and dwarfed Erskine Island like an eight-lane freeway around a pedestrian safety zone. Except that in this instance there was no safety.

'Now, ordinarily the currents around that way really pump', Ralph said.

> But around Christmas and New Year you get the strongest tides of the year and you can get anything up to 5 knots coming through there. I told them, 'You're just asking for trouble if you hold the comp there'.

Despite Ralph's protests the first day of competition remained scheduled for Erskine Island on 2 January.

> It didn't matter that we had a huge tide on the first day of the Australian Spearfishing Titles. No. All that seemed to matter was getting the swimming pool for underwater hockey. Everything had to work in around that. The bloody underwater hockey.

Still, there was no way Ralph Whalley was going to miss a national spearfishing championship, particularly one on his home turf. In fact, Ralph not only intended to take part, he intended to fully exploit the conditions and win.

In the months leading up to the 1983 competition, Ralph was trawling for prawns off North West Island. He'd be out there two weeks at a time, trawling at night, anchored up on a reef asleep during the day. He would stop by Erskine Island on his way to the fishing grounds and on his way back to Bundaberg. Sometimes he would dive Erskine reef, other times he would sit back on his boat, light a cigarette, crack open a beer and watch the tides moving around the tiny island.

'He just watches and works things out for himself. But there's no point asking him to explain what he knows because he can't', says his wife Anne.

The notion that someone could consider themselves capable of outwitting or even utilizing such a ferocious movement of water might seem insane. But it is by no means impossible. In his book *Bluewater Hunting and Freediving*, American spearfishing champion and writer Terry Maas describes in some detail how currents might affect a potential dive site and how 'bluewater hunters' can exploit currents to best advantage:

> Diving along a current-swept wall offers another opportunity to find favourable eddy currents (light currents flowing in the opposite direction of the strong prevailing current). Many times the area just ahead of, or behind, a small prominence projecting from a wall will offer a rest from the current and a place to ambush unsuspecting bluewater species.

Maas goes on to describe how he and his friends used such a current in a competition off Rhode Island, positioning themselves in the relative calm of an eddy current while spearing fish in a 6 knot current only 2 metres away.

Long before the 1983 competition took place Ralph had worked out that on a high tide he could dive the northern side of the reef, use the current to carry him back to Erskine, walk over to the other side of the island and dive the southern reef. That knowledge alone would place him at a significant advantage on the first day of competition. But Ralph also stumbled across a far more significant piece of information.

'The government were doing some type of study of the currents up there', he said.

> They were putting all these buoys in — plastic bags with a nail in the bottom and a bit of coolite on the top and a note in the bag saying, 'If found, return to us'. It was easy enough to pick one of these things out of the water every so often and see what was happening. What I found was the currents seemed to run back and forth along the same course.

Ralph stared at me expectantly for a few moments before realizing I hadn't understood.

'That means that if you get taken out by a current it will eventually bring you back to where you started', he said.

BRIEFING

I considered Sue Dockar was the top woman spearfisherman [sic] in this tournament ... I had no doubt that she would be able to cope with the prevailing conditions.

Ray Inkpen, statement to Queensland police, 3 January 1983

The first time Sue Dockar heard mention of the tides was at the briefing, the night before she disappeared. She had never dived any part of the Great Barrier Reef before, let alone Erskine Island. Her knowledge and skills were honed in cold, rough waters 1200 kilometres south. There she had learned to read that sea, to exploit the movement of the swell around headlands, predict southerly busters from a slight shift in the wind and waves. But this was no preparation for the subtle environmental cues of the tropics: the ominous calm of slack water moments before the current starts to run, the movement of reef fish in behind coral heads as they seek protection from the impending torrent and the pelagic hunters lying in wait. These were the cues a reef diver would look for: warnings to get out of the way or hang on for a wild ride.

Sue was not alone. Of the seventy-five spearos who took part in the 1983 competition, only a handful could claim any real diving experience on the Great Barrier Reef. Far fewer understood the current movements around the Capricorn and Bunker Groups and even they were in for a rude shock.

'No one expected the current to run like it did', was the assessment made by competitors and officials alike.

But that insight came after the event. The mood was very different as Australia's spearfishing elite crammed into Tanyella's communal dining room for their pre-competition briefing.

That evening, as they crowded around tables nursing tots of dark rum and cans of cold beer, the majority still talked about Erskine Island in terms of calm, clear blue water, coral trout and the opportunity to dive unencumbered by thick wetsuits and a belt full of lead. The main risk envisaged was that a reef shark might take a fancy to their catch.

Sue Dockar was as caught up in this image as everyone else. There she was, ensconced at a table with Greg at her side, surrounded by her friends, her team mates. In a matter of hours she would be diving the most famous stretch of reef in the world. Was she excited? Yes. Was she nervous? Of course — but that was good. It meant she was ready. She was serious.

Her concern was not so much the currents but her rivals.

'I think there were five, maybe six other women taking part in the competition', said Sue.

I can't say I knew them — they didn't go out of their way to talk to me and I'm not a great one for striking up a conversation. But I pretty much knew who was who, where they'd dived, what they'd won. The way I saw it, with six other girls in the comp that meant I had a one in seven chance of coming away with a national title. After that I started looking around the room, thinking, 'I can beat her. Not sure about her. I know I can beat her'.

Typically, she wasn't thinking so much of the shortfalls of others, rather the strengths within herself. That night, Sue's belief in her ability was stronger than it had ever been. She was ready for a hard day's diving and increasingly confident that she would go well.

It was around this time that Ray Inkpen squeezed a path through the crowd and took up position at a whiteboard at the front of the room. Ray waited for a while as conversation died away. He took a last look around the weather-beaten faces, making a final check of who was there and who was not.

First he announced that the charter boat, *Reefseeker*, would get under way around midnight. That meant all those travelling out on the vessel had to be at Gladstone's O'Connell wharf by 11 pm sharp. If anyone needed a lift up to Gladstone they should speak to him after the briefing.

All going well, *Reefseeker* would arrive at Erskine Island around 6.30 am and competition would commence at 7.00. The film fishing competition would follow at 1.30. Competitors would sleep overnight on Masthead Island where the second heat of the spearfishing competition would commence at 8 am the following day.

'Any questions so far?' asked Ray.

'Then he warned us about the tides', Sue recalls.

I knew the tides off Gladstone were big. Merv had warned us about them months ago. But this was the first I'd heard about how bad it was going to be. Ray said there was going to be a fair bit of current. I can't remember the exact words, just that we had to be careful and in an effort to work around the tides the first heat of the competition had been reduced from the usual six hours to four.

Sue remembers the shuffle of chairs and the muffled expletives from the back of the room. So does Ray. Before he walked into the dining room, he told himself it would not matter who he was or what he did, when you call the shots in spearfishing, you'd better have a short memory and darned thick hide. He had almost convinced himself that he didn't care what people thought. Yet years later he can still remember standing at that whiteboard, looking out at a sea of angry faces and steeling himself for the inevitable backlash.

'At that point the room just went off', says Sue.

People started shouting and swearing at Ray. It wasn't his fault. He was just the messenger. But I can understand the reaction. I was disappointed, but I also started to wonder how I would deal with the current. There was no way I would dive such conditions outside a competition, and I doubt anyone else in that room would either. But I looked around and I can tell you no one put their hand up and said the competition should be called off. Greg and I had come a long way. As I saw it, if that was the conditions on the day, well, the sea grants no favours, I would just have to get on with it like everyone else.

She watched Ray fielding the angry protests as best he could. No, they couldn't reschedule the spearfishing competition because other events also had to be considered. No, there was no chance of extending the time out on the reef. The schedule was too tight and the expected run on the tide too big.

Ray remembers one of his old mates from Western Australia shouting at him from the back of the room.

'If the run is as bad as you say are you going to have a helicopter on hand in case someone gets lost?' he demanded.

Murmurs spread around the room. Memories lingered of the previous national spearfishing titles at Five Fathom Bank near Perth. Halfway through the competition the Fremantle Doctor blew in and flat seas were transformed into washing machine conditions. Divers found themselves battling a 3 metre swell and a raging surface current to get back to the mother boat. Three hours later, and by that time several kilometres down-current, the last exhausted diver was plucked from the water by an Air Sea Rescue helicopter team.

Ray said there would be safety boats on hand. If anyone got into trouble, all they'd have to do was raise their speargun above their head and one of the boats would pick them up.

This statement was met with another wave of murmurs — the sound of negative information being cogitated and applied to each person's image of what diving on the Great Barrier Reef was all about. It was not until Ralph Whalley rose to his feet that the mood in the room began to settle.

Ralph picked up a marker pen and drew a simple map of Erskine Island and the surrounding bomboras on the whiteboard. Some people watched, others pulled out note pads and scribbled down the map.

A few of those present still remember the gist of what he said. Sue Dockar has the words inscribed somewhere deep inside her brain.

The main thing to remember is that the tide will run one way for a time, followed by a period of slack water, then it will turn and run back the other way. Like Ray said, if you get into trouble just raise your gun and wait for a safety boat to come and pick you up. Always remember that the tide will eventually bring you back to where you started.

When Ralph finished talking Ray got up again and announced that the safety boats would be leaving well after *Reefseeker*, departing at around 5.30 the following morning.

'There's a few places on the safety boats if anyone wants a ride out', he said.

Sue looked at Greg. He nodded. They put up their hands.

UNDER WAY

I believe in fate. I believe things happen for a reason.
Sue Dockar

There are a myriad of texts and neatly packaged conference papers explaining how fit, experienced, rational people can descend the path to mishap, disaster and tragedy. They describe events in terms of intricate emotional models, constructs of reality and 'sand pile effects' — all good material for the army of professionals and academics engaged in risk and disaster management. But people who make their living from the sea speak in plainer, more humble terms. Models and theories are of little use when a cyclone descends upon a vessel and there is no land in sight. Then it is all about preparation, anticipation and — some would argue — two factors that, despite the best efforts of our scientific community, cannot be quantified or rationalized.

Intuition and luck have been part of life on the sea since the first dug-out canoe was launched through the surf. Don't whistle on a boat; never put your left foot down first when boarding a ship; live rabbits and clothed women aboard a vessel bring bad luck; and sighting a flat-footed person or a red-haired woman before a vessel leaves port is sure to bring disaster. All this might sound irrelevant in an age when, among other things, luxury liners set sail every day carrying their share of flat-footed, red-headed, fully clothed women. But when you are in a small boat and the sky turns black, a flat sea turns into an alpine landscape and the wind rips tears from your eyes, intuition and luck suddenly become very important in your life.

'Ralph's father was unbelievable', says Anne. 'Ralph's like it now. He'll see ducks fly over and say, "It's going to rain in two days time". Or, "Three days of fog and you'll get rain". Or, "Don't take bananas on a fishing boat".'

'Black cats', said Ralph.

If I see a black cat on the way to work I may as well turn around and come home. I make no money, it costs me a fortune and brings me all the trouble under the sun. Black cats. Arrgghh! They should be banned.

Ralph knew something was going to happen back in 1983. But it had nothing to do with intuition or luck. Putting divers in the water on a big tide was asking for trouble, simple as that. Ralph knew the waters. He'd warned of what was to come. But no one was listening. In less than an hour *Reefseeker* would be heading out to Erskine Island with fifty divers aboard. In six hours time he and twenty-four others would head out there too. Ralph stubbed out his cigarette and retired to his bunk.

'She was lit up like a Christmas tree.' That was Vlado's first impression of the large steel catamaran tied up at Gladstone's O'Connell wharf. It was 10.45 pm. Blabster had dropped the four NSW juniors off at the wharf while he parked the car. The boys were standing together with their dive buckets and swags, trying hard not to look excited, as if going out and diving the reef was something quite normal in their lives. Truth be known, it would be the first time any of them had dived from a charter vessel; the first time they had been more than a few kilometres offshore.

'Before that I think the largest boat any of us had been on was Merv's 5 metre Haines', says Vlado.

For those times, *Reefseeker* was impressive. At around 18 metres long and 8.5 metres wide, she dwarfed other charter boats tied up along the creek that night. Her main deck consisted of a large lounge-come-dining room and galley, flanked by a series of bunk rooms. The lounge opened onto a wide aft deck where benches ran along each gunwale and a narrow platform, or duckboard, hung from the stern so that divers could step down into the sea and climb back on board with comparative ease. A flight of metal stairs ran from the aft deck to the upper deck where the crews quarters and wheelhouse were situated. If *Reefseeker* had a fault it was speed — or the lack of it. Even with her engines working at full power *Reefseeker*'s top speed was only 7 knots, making her one of the slowest charter vessels working the reef.

But that was of no concern for the four NSW juniors. At the time all they wanted was to get on board and claim a bunk — Mark for one needed to do the trip lying down so that he wouldn't spend the next six hours puking over the side. When Blabster finally arrived they quickly gathered up their gear and hurried up the gangplank.

'Someone was standing there taking names as we came aboard — I think it was Ray Inkpen', says Vlado.

Anyway, Blabster told us to stow our dive gear out on the main deck. Then we charged in and dumped our swags in one of the bunk rooms.

There were a lot of people on the boat and the mood was good, like a party mood — all of us were looking forward to getting out and diving the reef. Us four went up on the top deck and when we finally got under way I remember looking out at the lights around the harbour and thinking, 'Far out, we're really doing this, it's really happening!'

A bit later Mark and Scottie went down and found the older guys had turfed our gear off the bunks. They ended up sleeping on the floor in the lounge. Lennie and me, we sat up on the top deck for most of the night playing poker. On the stroke of midnight I said, 'It's my birthday'. Lennie said, 'What do you know, it's my birthday too'. He said, 'Hey, how about that? Happy birthday!' and I said 'Happy birthday' back and we kept on playing.

Sue Dockar lay next to her sleeping husband watching the minutes tick by on Greg's watch, waiting for 4 am. It had been a restless night. Her mind was busy building pictures of Erskine Island, attempting to bring context to Ralph's advice. But even though sleep had been elusive, she felt calm and alert.

From outside the room she could hear the belches and groans of men stirred prematurely from slumber, the noises of dive gear being stuffed into holdalls, of bare feet padding across the verandah. She fumbled around on the bedside locker for the light switch and her glasses.

While Greg stirred and stretched, Sue put on her bikini, team T-shirt and shorts, then brushed her hair into place. Her speargun, dive gear and rig were neatly stowed in a dive bucket next to the door, along with sleeping bags and a change of clothes for an overnight stay on Masthead Island. Greg pulled on his clothes and put his arms around Sue. They stood at the doorway and hugged for a while, then walked out into the cool morning air.

Pre-comp meals are a pivotal part of any dive preparation. According to studies conducted by the University of California, the average freediver on a relaxed dive burns 5000 kilojoules per hour. That is higher than any other activity apart from fast axe-chopping. Multiply this by four to six hours of hard competition and you have a phenomenal energy requirement. But the diver also has to contend with water pressure. A cubic centimetre of water weighs

1 gram. One cubic metre of water weighs a metric tonne and as the diver descends, pressure on the body increases, distorting the stomach and oesophagus. Too much food too close to the dive can invoke the curse of heartburn and stomach cramps, making freediving an uncomfortable, perhaps even painful experience.

As one might expect, various formulas have evolved balancing the need for energy with the unique physiology of freediving. Maas recommends a carbohydrate loading of around 8400 kilojoules drawn from pastas, breads, vegetables and fruits the night before the dive, followed by a light breakfast in the hours prior. This, he claims, should stand the diver in good stead for the next few hours. Nevertheless, there are highly competent divers who swear by a full cooked breakfast, hash browns, sausages and all. And then there's Ralph Whalley, his cigarette and the infamous bottle of Stone's Green Ginger Wine.

The whiteboard displaying Ralph's crude map of Erskine Island still stood at the far end of the dining room when Sue and Greg arrived; a silent reminder of the briefing only a few hours prior. Barefooted men sat around beer-stained tables, hunched over bowls of cereal and steaming cups, their sleepy faces haggard in the harsh glare of fluorescent light.

Sue and Greg nodded a few hellos as they went over to the kitchen. Greg found a frying pan in one of the cupboards and proceeded to fry up eggs, bacon and tomatoes. A few of the divers looked on.

'Jesus Greg. It's four in the morning!'

But as far as Greg was concerned he wasn't diving and it was going to be a long time till lunch. So he shrugged and munched on a slice of bread while the smell of frying bacon filled the room. For Sue, a piece of toast and mug of tea would have to suffice until the competition was out of the way.

'I never eat much before a dive. That morning I had a stomach full of butterflies which pretty much killed my appetite anyway. It was pure excitement', she says.

Not that all but those closest to her would have been able to tell. Sue Dockar is not predisposed to emotional outbursts. Before a competition her friends notice she becomes more intent, more focused. Her head might turn a little quicker when she's asked a question. Sometimes she even frowns.

But excited she was. Sue was about to fulfil a childhood dream. Deep inside she was feeling the same adrenaline rush, the dump wave of excitement and anticipation that had seen Mark, Lennie and Vlado bounce onto *Reefseeker* like excited puppies.

Sue and Greg sat down at a table with a few of the others from the NSW team. No one spoke much. Then again, who does at 4 am?

Sitting nearby was Ralph Whalley, Tim Paulsen, the clean-cut Paul Welsby and Andy Ruddock, whose reputation was as wild and unruly as the mop of curls that cascaded down his back. Two other men had dive gear spread across the table and floor. They were in deep concentration, one man re-threading a line to his spear, the other securing his dive buoy to his rig. 'Some people can do that and it doesn't faze them', Sue says. 'For me, there would be nothing worse than checking my gear at the last moment and finding something was broken or missing. I just can't do it. I can't cross my fingers and hope for the best.'

After breakfast Sue and Greg went back to their room, picked up their bags and headed down to the car park. The world seemed so peaceful in the pre-dawn grey. Even the breeze held soft warmth. The rest of the safety boat party congregated around the cars. Ralph and a couple of other men from the Queensland team had climbed into the trailered boats and were busy stowing the spearguns, dive buckets and bags as they were handed up.

There were five safety boats in all: two 6 metre Shark Cats — one owned by Ralph Whalley, the other by professional fisherman Don Norman; a 6 metre Seafarer, property of Cairns dentist Rod Ashton; an 8 metre Hydrofield belonging to cane farmer John Powell; and a 7 metre Haines Hunter, the pride and joy of panel beater and pub owner Gerry Hill. Motors ranged from single 120 horsepower through to twin 200 horsepower. In reasonable conditions, the boats were capable of cutting a course 70 to 120 kilometres out to the reef and back in a day with a few good dives in between.

Around 4.30 am, the last piece of gear was stowed and people crowded into the cars. Sue Dockar managed to get a seat in the back of John Powell's four-wheel drive, wedged in the middle. There was not enough space for everyone, so Greg and a few of the others climbed up onto the trailers and rode in the boats.

The convoy pulled out of Tanyella and wove its way up the hill, past Tannum Sands Hotel and in towards Gladstone. It was a thirty minute drive for a car towing a boat — plenty of time to get to the ramp. Then, with a few willing hands to get the boats in the water, the gear secure, and the cars and trailers parked, they should be off by 5.30 am. That was the plan: a plan that would have given plenty of time for the safety boat party to rendezvous with *Reefseeker* by 7.30 and start the competition at 8.00. Trouble was, when they arrived at the boat ramp what they found was a bare concrete slope standing in mud.

On any other day, the low tide would merely have been an inconvenience. But on 2 January 1983, timing was everything. Some swore, some made jokes, but in the grand scheme of things their comments were irrelevant. The tide they had worked so hard to out-manoeuvre trumped them before they even got in the water.

Sue and Greg sat down with a few of the others on the boat ramp. One man pulled out a pack of cards and started playing solitaire on the concrete. A couple of others got up and went for a walk along the waterfront. Sue looked out over the mud and watched the wind blow soft ripples across the creek. 'All we could do was wait for the tide to come back in.'

But the look on Ralph's face bothered her. His famous larrikin humour was noticeably absent. She watched him light a cigarette, wander down the boat ramp and look out to sea. He stood there for a long time.

Ralph read much more into that exposed mud than he cared to — years later he confessed that even he had not expected the tide to be that low. And as all fishermen know, a tide acts like a pendulum: the harder it swings one way, the harder and faster it comes back. An extremely low tide meant an extremely high tide would follow. Then there was the weather — the sky was already overcast and the wind was picking up. If it had been a social dive, Ralph probably would have called off the trip then and there. But it was the national championships. People were depending on them. They had to get out to the reef.

More than an hour passed before the water was high enough to launch the boats. One by one the cars reversed down the ramp and the boats were unhitched from their trailers and pushed unceremoniously into the water.

Sue followed Don Norman's boat down the ramp with Paul Welsby, helped push it out onto the water and climbed on board. Greg waded out with Gerry's boat then hauled himself over the gunwales. Gerry turned the ignition switch and the boat let out a deep-throated roar, the noise shattering the peace of early morning. The other boats roared into life and nosed their way into the main channel. Greg knew he should be feeling good. After all, they were finally under way. But he sensed trouble.

I'd been around the spearfishing circuit long enough to know these guys pushed their boats hard. The low tide had taken everyone by surprise and put us well behind schedule. I may not be a spearo, but one thing I did know was they would be out to make up lost time. It was going to be a rough trip out.

It was around 6.30 am when the boats passed the last channel marker and met the open sea. Greg remembers the feeling of exhilaration as Gerry jammed the throttle down and the dog clutch snapped in. The boat surged forward, rising up and planing across the waves. He gripped the gunwale, bent his knees ready for the impact of the waves. Horsepower throbbed under his bare feet, salt spray hit his face like a thousand tiny needles.

For a while Greg thought his fears had been misplaced. There they were, screaming out to sea, five boats abreast. He would tell his friends about this when they got back to Sydney: the wild boat trip out to the reef with the crazy Queenslanders.

Greg was standing next to the windscreen when they slammed into the wave. He remembers the high-pitched squeal as the propellers came clear of the water, the green-blue wave rushing towards them like a Mack truck, and the sickening noise of glass shattering under sudden and extreme pressure. He braced himself for pain as the glass-encrusted wave flew up above him and exploded onto the boat. The next thing he remembers is Gerry pulling back hard on the throttles, bringing the boat to an abrupt halt. Then he turned to survey the damage.

'I don't know how, but every piece of glass flew over the top of me and hit the guy standing behind me', Greg says.

> He was pretty badly cut and there was a piece of glass in his eye. All the boats stopped at that point. They came over to see if we were OK and ask if they could help. We spent the next hour sitting on the swell picking pieces of glass up out of the boat and trying to wash the glass out of this guy's eye with sea water.

They were now an hour behind schedule with a damaged boat, an injured man and five barefooted men standing on a deck covered in broken glass.

> I remember Gerry just shook his head and said, 'I've got a really bad feeling about this comp'. At the time I didn't read too much into the low tide, the broken windscreen and the guy with glass in his eye. I'm not superstitious, but looking

back I ask myself whether it was just nature's way of saying, 'Go home. Today is not your day'.

It was another half hour before the boats were under way again. Waves were coming at them in short, sharp sets, making the trip decidedly uncomfortable, particularly for Gerry Hill and his passengers, now without the protection of a windscreen.

Over on Don Norman's boat, Sue Dockar was holding onto the steel rail under the windscreen. The constant jarring was taking a toll on her arms and legs. Even so, she struck up a conversation with Don and Ray Oakey, the fireman from Brisbane. They told her about the fish she could expect to see at Erskine Island: coral trout, sweetlip, mangrove jack, trevally, spangled emperor and coral cod. Occasionally, Don would point to something in the distance — an eagle ray, or a school of dolphins, or a turtle basking on the surface. And as they travelled further out to sea she watched the colour of the waves change from muddy blue, to sapphire, to turquoise.

The boats swept past Polmaise Reef — the first major reef in the Capricorn Group. Waves boomed up against the coral. Don told her Polmaise dropped away to 20 metres on the southern side and around to the north-east it formed one side of a deep channel with nearby Masthead Island. The funnelling action of the channel added an extra knot or so to the tidal movement. Don said Ralph and Tim had spent a fair bit of time diving Polmaise. They didn't talk much about the view, or the currents. All Ralph would say was that it was good fishing but the tiger sharks 'followed you around like dogs'.

The seas flattened out as they came into the lee of the reef. Throttles went down and the boats hurtled on across the waves. A few moments later, Sue caught her first glimpses of green on the horizon.

As we came closer I could make out this tall bank of trees coming up out of the sea. I thought it must be Erskine Island but then Don shouted out that we were coming up to Masthead. We were really moving by that stage. I remember one minute Masthead seemed miles away, then our boats were screaming past this long stretch of reef just out from the island. I could see the white sand on the beach and the trunks of the trees. For a brief moment I thought how good it would be to just slow down and take a closer look. But there was no time. All of a sudden Masthead was behind us and Don was shouting again and pointing dead ahead.

I looked forward and I could see a large boat anchored next to this tiny patch of scrub. It looked like one of those islands you see in cartoons. You know: the one just big enough for the castaway to sit under the coconut palm. I thought, 'There's no way that can be Erskine Island!' but that's where we were going.

My next thought was of Ralph's mud map of the reef and bombies. I tried to transpose that map onto what I was looking at. My plan was to head out from Erskine on the slack tide and gradually fish my way back as the current increased. But at that stage I had no starting point as such, or any idea where the best fishing spots lay.

Don was helpful. He slowed down as we came closer and pointed out a couple of bombies around to the north-east of the island. I looked down into the water and could see coral only a few metres below. Don reckoned we'd find some good fish in the area.

I made a mental note of where it was in relation to Erskine and thought, 'Right, that's where I'm heading'.

LIKE CLOCKWORK

If you think you can win, you can.

William Hazlitt, On Great and Little Things

They were late. The words Ray Inkpen did not want to hear that morning drummed on his nerves. He rested his elbows on *Reefseeker*'s gunwales and stared out to sea, willing the five safety boats to appear on the horizon. Occasionally sunlight would play on a white-crested wave, creating the illusion of wake from a boat. But as much as he squinted and frowned into the distance, as much as he cursed the weather, there were no boats to be seen.

Reefseeker had been anchored off Erskine Island for close to two hours. As everyone seemed so keen to remind him, the competition should have been under way by now. Instead, the sky was overcast, the sea was unsettled and he had a bunch of ill-tempered spearos looking at him as if he was somehow responsible for the weather and the delay.

Ray had expected some degree of high-spirited chaos in the run-up to the competition. It was almost a tradition that something would go wrong, or someone would be claiming the event was rigged in favour of the home team. But this was different. It didn't seem to matter what he did or how hard he tried, it was beginning to feel as though the competition was jinxed.

He turned his back on the sea and climbed *Reefseeker*'s metal stairs up to the wheelhouse. Merv Sheehan and a few of the other officials were crowded into the cabin with *Reefseeker*'s skipper, Doug Walkden. They were poring over a chart, trying to figure out where the five safety boats might be. Everyone present had a theory on why they were late. One of the boats could have run up on a reef or broken down. Or Ralph could have got them all drunk and they were too hungover to get the boats in the water.

'No chance, Ralph would still make the comp', someone said.

But Ray's main concern was not the safety boats as such. For him, the big issue was timing. From the outset, the Queensland officials had known that if the event was to run at all it had to run like clockwork. In their minds if the competition had started on time they would have had a good two and a half hours of slack water before the tide turned. The delay was steadily eroding that period of grace. Now, their options were limited. They could not start the competition without the safety boats. First, it would be madness to put divers in the open sea without some means of picking them up in an emergency. Second, the safety boat party included five of the top divers in the home team. There was no way the Queensland officials would start the competition without them.

Years later and with the luxury of hindsight, Ray Inkpen wondered why they didn't see conditions for what they were and call the event off. But on 2 January 1983, the mood aboard *Reefseeker* was uncompromising. As Ray was painfully aware, people had come from all around Australia to compete in a national championship. No one particularly cared why the safety boats were late, that the tide was much bigger than expected, or that sea conditions were deteriorating fast.

'Things had gone too far', he says now. 'If I had walked out of that wheelhouse and announced the competition was cancelled I would have been lynched.'

There was a brief sense of relief when he sighted the approaching safety boats at around 8.30 am. But if he thought their arrival signalled an end to the morning's dramas he was mistaken.

First, Gerry Hill brought his boat around the stern of *Reefseeker* and Ray saw the broken windscreen and a man holding a bloodstained T-shirt to his face. Then Don Norman arrived and said one of his engines was playing up — fuel-line trouble. And then there was Ralph.

Instead of coming directly alongside he motored around to the north-east of Erskine, occasionally letting the boat drift with the swell, an act that sparked a storm of protest on *Reefseeker*.

'Several competitors claimed Ralph was scouting the area', says Ray. 'Now that's quite normal and sensible on a social dive, but it's a hanging offence in competitive spearfishing and they wanted Ralph disqualified.'

Ralph says he was doing no such thing. He was just checking the position of *Reefseeker* against the run of the tide, and he didn't like what he saw: the tide was going to run from north-west to south-east, and *Reefseeker* was moored to the south of the island. In his opinion that gave the vessel protection from the swell but would leave it exposed to the full force of the tide.

And then there was the other part of the equation. The previous evening Ralph had told the divers that the most extensive part of Erskine's fringing reef and the best fishing lay to the north and east of the island. Logic would dictate that was where the majority of divers would head. But the north-east side of the reef would also be fully exposed to the tide. He knew that with *Reefseeker* anchored to the south of Erskine, any diver caught in the current would have no hope of getting back to the boat.

Ralph pushed the throttles down and motored over to *Reefseeker*, determined to talk some sense into them.

'I wanted the skipper to move the boat down to the eastern lee of the island. That would have given some protection from the current and meant divers could have drifted back to the boat', he says.

But when Ralph came alongside no one wanted to hear about his concerns.

'There was a lot of shouting going on and Ralph was getting worked up', recalls Merv Sheehan. 'The guys making the protest were from my team so I weighed in. I told them Ralph was just trying to do the right thing. I said he'd dived the area all his life. He didn't need to cheat.'

In the end the protests were quashed and Ralph was allowed to compete. But the clock was ticking, nerves were frayed and the element of trust and goodwill which bonded many spearos had been superseded by the urge to win. Far worse, the protest effectively doused the last opportunity organizers had to mitigate the impact of the tide: namely, by moving the boat. It is unclear whether Ralph's concerns ever reached *Reefseeker*'s skipper, but the vessel remained at anchor for the duration of the competition. The near-fatal consequences would be played out over the next three days.

Sue knew nothing of Ralph's concerns. By the time he came alongside *Reefseeker*, Don Norman had brought their boat in to shore at Erskine Island.

We geared up on the boat. I just had a skivvy to keep the sun off, plus a wetsuit long john. Merv was really concerned about sunburn, so I made a point of plastering my face and the backs of my hands with blockout and zinc. Then someone handed me the sign-on sheet. I scribbled my name, the date and passed it on.

Once we were geared up, Don brought the boat up to the beach and dropped us off. Even though it was overcast, I remember feeling hot and uncomfortable. I jumped over the side and just sat in the water for a while. I can't say it was refreshing, like jumping into the sea back home, but it cooled me down a bit.

I remember wading ashore and thinking how small the island was. It was just a steep beach with a patch of coarse scrub in the middle — you could literally walk around it in a few minutes. Then I looked across at Masthead Island. I don't know what the distance was but it looked close, 3 maybe 4 kilometres away. I walked around to the northern side of the island. There was a long spit of sand. I walked out as far as I could and stood there for a while trying to get my bearings. I could make out the edge of the reef and figured the bombie Don had shown us to be another 500 metres or so further out.

I went back to the southern side of the island. Most of the teams and officials were ashore by that stage. Ray and Merv were busy setting up the starting pen. All the divers were kitted up and ready to go. From then on we were all told to stay down the southern end of the island.

From what I can recall, around 9.10 Ray gave one last briefing. He wanted us to allow plenty of time to get back to the boat. Anyone caught out by the current was to raise their gun and wait for a safety boat to come and get them. Then Ray called, 'One minute'.

I remember Greg was standing with Merv, and I went over and handed him my glasses. He gave me a kiss and wished me luck. He had a bottle of water so I took a last drink then I filed into the starting pen with everyone else. I tried my best to look calm, but my mouth was dry and my stomach was turning. I put on my face mask, and the corrective lenses brought everything back into focus. I took a quick look around at the other competitors. Everyone looked pretty intense.

Ray called: 'Thirty seconds'. There was a bit of pushing as we began to move forward towards the sea. I looked across the beach at the waves gently breaking on the shore and tried to picture the fish I'd been talking about with Ray and Don as we'd travelled out in the boat. I looked across at Greg. He smiled at me and winked. Then the whistle blew.

At 9.20 am on Sunday 2 January, the 1983 National Spearfishing Titles finally commenced. To any onlooker it was chaos. People shouting and pushing, some running up the beach, others diving straight into the sea, their precious spearguns and rigs gripped firmly under their arms. But each had a path mapped out. Each one was focused on the hunt; each one out to win.

Sue Dockar ran along the beach and around to the northern side of the island. This was always the worst part of any competition for her: running along a beach in a wetsuit. Even her facemask trapped perspiration which trickled into her eyes as she ran. But she kept running until she reached the northernmost tip of the sandbar.

Once I got my bearings I ran into the waves, pulled on my fins and loaded my speargun. I remember swimming out hard and keeping up that pace as the sea floor started to drop away. All the butterflies had gone. I felt capable of winning. All I had to do was stay focused and have faith in myself.

It would be two days before she touched land again.

THE TIDE TURNS

What do you think about in a comp? You think about how
deep the water is and how many times you can dive down
without incurring shallow water blackout. You think about
where other divers are and where you are in relation to
them. You think about where your main rivals are and
whether they will get better fish than you. You wonder if
you should have followed them and attempted to out-dive
them or trust your own knowledge and instincts.
You think about winning.

Mark Colys

With the luxury of hindsight, it seems ironic that the start of the
competition was greeted with a sense of relief by Ray Inkpen, Merv
Sheehan — even Greg Dockar. They had just watched seventy-five
divers, including friends and loved ones, charge headlong into the
open sea, in the full knowledge that one of the strongest tides of the
year was about to run. But no one believed that the disaster Ralph
Whalley had predicted could really unfold.

All Ray, Merv and Greg saw were clear blue waves rolling
gently over the reef. All they knew was that for the first time in a

long time there was no one to organize, no one to placate, no rendezvous to keep.

They climbed into one of the safety boats and headed back to *Reefseeker*. It was time to kick back a little: to take in the sun and be lulled into thinking things were running smoothly. Even *Reefseeker*'s two deckhands took a break from their duties to hang fishing lines off the ship's stern.

Ray Inkpen reckoned there would be an hour or so before the first of the divers arrived to weigh in their fish. He did not intend to waste that opportunity. He set up the weigh-in scales and tally sheets on *Reefseeker*'s aft deck. Then, at around 10.15 am, he put on his wetsuit and weight belt, carried his fins, mask and gun to *Reefseeker*'s stern. He pulled his mask strap over his head, put on his fins and took one last look around.

The water looked reasonably calm and tantalizingly blue. And even though the sky was overcast, rays of sunlight slipped through, giving harsh brilliance to the waves. Divers and their floats peppered the reef and outlying bomboras. There were no spearguns raised in signs of distress, no one swimming back to *Reefseeker* unable to cope with the conditions.

Ray picked up his speargun, strode out from the boat and plunged into the sea. He hung in the water for a moment, checked his line, then swam out towards the reef.

'I thought we'd gotten away with it', he says.

Andy Ruddock can still recall when he joined the Wollongong Kingfishers Spearfishing Club. He was eleven years old.

> They looked after me. They brought me up. I used to go along when the club competed in the Alliman and the Taylor Shields. It was the old school: until you could spear good fish that would help them win a comp you didn't get a boat ride. If you were a lowly junior like I was you just went in off the rocks.

It was close to six years before Andy was offered a boat ride. He can still picture the boat — a 4 metre ply vessel with a 55 horsepower Archimedes outboard motor. On the day in question, Andy arrived early, placed his gear in the boat and, full of pride and anticipation, went up to the Kingfisher's dive marshal and wrote his name on the club sign-on sheet.

> Two minutes before the start of the comp, Peter Idle turned up and I was told he was going out in the boat instead of me. Peter was an A grade diver and I was only a C grader. He was more likely to get fish to help the club win so he got my place.

By 1983, Andy was twenty-seven years old and the boy who couldn't get a boat ride had become one of the toughest, most tenacious spearos in Australia. He had speared competitively in every Australian state. He'd dived for pearls off Broome, beche de mere in the Torres Strait. He'd dived with hammerhead and tiger sharks and hunted game fish in the Coral Sea. What made him so good? Some said he had no fear.

Andy disagrees.

> To me there's a difference between competence and stupidity. There are heaps of divers who are fitter and dive deeper than me. I don't take the risks they take or push myself anywhere near as hard. But I get respect because over a six-hour comp I can keep up with them. It is my fish knowledge and adaptability that beats a lot of the other guys.

Andy approached the 1983 championships in the same way he approached every spearfishing competition: he spent three days diving nearby reefs — in this case, Polmaise, Fitzroy and Lamont. Ideally, he would have spent some time diving Erskine Island too, getting a feel for the water and acquainting himself with the local fish. But the opportunity never came up, so Andy did the next best thing. On the way out to the reef he picked the brains of his friend, rival and drinking buddy Ralph Whalley.

The main thing I remember was Ralph bitching about the currents. That's all he went on about on the way out to Erskine. We talked through a few dive scenarios for the comp, but it always came back to currents. In the end Ralph reckoned he was going to dive to the north-west of Erskine and turn back early. He knew the area better than most so I decided that I'd do the same.

While the majority of competitors raced across Erskine Island and out to the north-eastern stretch of reef, Andy Ruddock walked around to the western tip. 'I don't run. Running burns me out.'

He waded into the turquoise sea, put on his mask and fins, loaded the spear onto the stock, pulled the rubber back over the catch and headed out.

Sixteen years of competitive spearfishing had taught Andy two things: take nothing for granted and rely on no one. Even so, as he paddled around to the north-western side of the reef he looked forward to catching up with Ralph.

Andy watched the waves for Ralph's fishing float. He dropped down and cruised around the coral heads, came back up to the surface and checked the waves once more, but he could not find his friend. No matter. He turned his attention to a cave nestled behind a bank of coral, figuring their paths were bound to cross sometime in the next four hours.

He figured wrong.

It took Sue Dockar a good half hour to swim out to her target bombora, a moderate swim in spearfishing terms. Time enough for her mind to settle and her lungs to expand. She followed a compass bearing, swimming north-north-east — a course which took her over magnificent gardens of staghorn coral and intricate gorgonian fans. Outside competition Sue would have had time to watch the tiny brightly coloured fairy basslets darting around pink, lilac and honey coloured corals, or notice the sea star the colour of purest sapphire and the texture of suede. But Sue was diving to win. In that black and white world, she viewed the reef in terms of where she would find fish, how they would move and where they would hide. Over sand she watched for spangled emperor; around the delicate, kaleidoscopic reef she was on the hunt for coral trout, job fish, parrot fish and wrasse. And when she finally saw the bombora looming ahead in the blue haze she paused, not to appreciate the seascape, but to take a very clinical 360 degree scan.

> The water was 7, may be 8 metres deep, visibility was around 15 metres and there was a mild swell coming in from the east. I couldn't feel any current. I could see divers off to the south-west of me but no one close by. For me that was good, so I dived down and started to fish.
>
> The main thing on my mind was how the fish were going to react to me and the gun. Some fish are real skittish. They see a diver and they're gone. Other fish will stick around. On a social day you have time to weigh things up. In a comp you have to get a handle on things straight away. You take the skittish ones first.

She moved slowly, checking under coral ledges, in caves and crevices. After each dive she would rest on the surface, watching the fish move below her, working out her next move. Then she would drop back down again, and again, and again.

Until now her average dive had been around 10 metres, her breathhold ranged somewhere between 30 and 60 seconds: small change in the world of freediving. But competitive spearfishing is more about pace and endurance. Back in Sydney, that dive profile meant she could spend around two hours of a six-hour competition underwater. In the warm, shallow waters off Erskine Island, with the incentive of a national title, her bottom time steadily increased.

'You get focused. If there is a fish down there you hang on a bit longer, if not, you go up and rest. After a while you don't think about breathing. All you think about is the fish', said Sue.

Finally Sue noticed a slight movement under a plate coral. She swam a little closer until she could make out the striped body and scarlet fins of a red-throated emperor. For a few moments Sue settled on the coral. Then she approached, careful not to make any sudden move or to look directly at the fish. She managed to get within a few metres before it appeared concerned by her presence. By then the dull twang of rubber had already signalled its demise.

In any competitive arena, first blood — be it measured in a point, goal or set — is a significant moment. It boosts confidence, reassures and encourages the competitor they have what it takes to win. For Sue, that momentary elation came on the surface, when she stabbed her knife into the struggling creature's brain and snapped back its neck. But as soon as the fish was on her rig it was back to business. She reloaded the spear into the shaft, pulled the rubbers over the catch and dropped back under the water.

Above her, the lifeless fish rose and fell with the waves, the olive green stripes on its body glittering in the daylight, one black and gold eye staring up at the sun. Each wave pushed it further along the rigline towards Sue's bright orange fishing buoy.

Around 10.15 am, Sue thought she heard a helicopter flying overhead: possibly a charter flight taking tourists out to Heron Island. If the passengers had looked down, they would have seen divers scattered around Erskine's reefs and outlying shoals like ants foraging on discarded cake. They could have seen Sue's buoy at the end of her rigline. If the tidal predictions for that day were correct, it should have been slack tide at that time. On a slack tide there would be no current and the rigline hangs loosely behind the diver. Instead, the line had curled around from the west and was gradually stretching out east-south-east. It was a subtle movement; one that Sue noted but paid little heed to at the time. The current was starting to run.

There are complex calculations, equations and graphs that can be used to illustrate the movement between high and low water. But the simplest explanation is to compare it to a child on a swing. From the moment you push the child away, momentum starts to build. That momentum peaks as the swing sweeps past the ground and steadily diminishes as the child's feet race towards the sky. The harder you push, the greater the range and velocity of the movement. But the momentum always peaks midway between the two extremes.

On much of the Great Barrier Reef the sea oscillates between high and low tide every six hours or so. During the first hour, the movement, known as a tidal stream, is gentle and slow. In the second hour the velocity of the tidal stream steadily increases. The greatest movement of water, and therefore the strongest tidal stream, occurs in the third and fourth hours, midway between high and low water. By the fifth hour the volume of water has diminished and the momentum gradually falls away. By the sixth hour, the volume and power of the tidal stream is spent. It is low water. For an hour or so, mangroves, mudflats and coral stand proud of the waves and sea birds probe shallow pools for molluscs and stranded fish. Then it begins again.

Around the Capricorn Group, local fishermen have learned to factor in a few variables. First, tidal movements are strongest in the deep channel areas between the cays. Second, low pressure systems such as those which occur in Queensland's cyclone season, increase the height and run on a tide. They may also increase or decrease the interval between high and low waters by as much as two hours, but perhaps more significantly, they may cause the tidal stream to pick up speed much faster and with much greater intensity than usual.

At these times you might as well rip up your tide tables and throw them in the bin.

On 2 January 1983 there was a 4.67 metre tide and two low pressure systems — one over the mainland, the other over the sea to the north of the Capricorn Group. That combination was the equivalent of pushing a swing with every ounce of energy possible.

Seventy-five divers were in the water. Those furthest from land, close to the deep channel between Erskine and Heron Islands, would be most at risk. Sue Dockar was 500 to 600 metres north-north-east of Erskine Island. At this point, she could still have freestyled back to the comparative safety of the shallows, albeit with only one fish on her rig. But in the clear blue water the only thing on Sue's mind was winning.

By 10.30 am, Andy Ruddock had made his way around to the northern side of the reef about a kilometre north of Erskine Island. 'I was there with Gerry Hill. What with the currents and everything we decided to stick together for a while and we got a few fish. But there was this mangrove jack …'

Mangrove jack is a beautiful, hard-fighting fish that grows up to 12 kilograms. Some know it as dog bream because of its powerful dog-like front teeth which have sunk into the hands and arms of many an unsuspecting angler. This said, mangrove jack will sooner flee than fight. And even though this particular fish was safely ensconced in a channel under the bombora, too tight and too long for any human to access, it took one look at the masked face of Andy Ruddock and bolted to the far end of its sanctuary.

'Gerry was diving on the other side of the bombie', said Andy.

He came up and said, 'Did you see that jack?' I said, 'Yeah!' I dived down and it would bolt over one side of the channel and he'd dive down and it would bolt over the other. This went on for ages. In the end we both dived down together so the jack would have nowhere to go. After all that neither of us got it.

Somewhere around that time Andy felt the current start to run. It was the slightest of movements, but he remembered Ralph's warning.

'That was only an hour or so into the competition. I said to Gerry, "I'm heading back or else I'm not going to make it". He said, "Yeah, I'll just fish a little bit longer".'

'Gerry didn't make it back [unassisted]. I did.'

Merv Sheehan pushed aside a few dive buckets and sat down on a long steel bench close to *Reefseeker*'s stern. He wore the same short-sleeved blue polo shirt and baggy blue shorts as the rest of the NSW team. The only difference in his uniform was the blue jacket lying on the seat next to him. Most such jackets boasted a few professionally embroidered red and gold crests, each marking attendance at a national spearfishing title. On Merv's, lines of crests ran from the chest to the waist. They told the world that since 1960, Merv Sheehan had attended just about every national spearfishing championships held in Australia, first as a competitor, in later years as team manager. It told competitors and officials alike that he'd been spearing fish while most of them were still in nappies.

To Merv, the weighing-in of fish was a serious business; a task demanding complete concentration, precision and a degree of ceremony. Get it right and each diver's skill, knowledge and stamina was acknowledged; order and hierarchy were re-established; everyone walked away happy. Get it wrong and friendships, not to mention noses, could be broken, feuds born. Merv Sheehan had seen it all.

Officially, he had no role in the 1983 weigh-in. That honour went to Queensland high school teacher Mike McDade. As weigh-master, it was Mike's role to announce the species and weight of the fish after the diver placed the fish on the scales. It was up to him to resolve any disputes should a fish be undersize. Assistant weigh-master Graham Henderson from Victoria would consult the score table and calculate the point value of each fish: one hundred points for each eligible fish caught, plus ten points per kilo with a minimum weight of 1 kilo. Another assistant weigh-master, in this instance Greg Dockar, would record the results and announce the final score.

Concerns about shark activity had spurred the organizers to opt for a progressive weigh-in. In other words, rather than weigh all the fish in at the end of the competition, a diver could swim back to *Reefseeker* at any time, have their catch weighed and placed on ice, then plunge back into the sea and fish some more. Granted, weighing-in fish would cost the diver time out of the competition, but it meant a hard day's fishing would make it to the scales. No one liked losing good fish to a shark.

Merv had full view of the spring-balanced scales hanging from a steel beam traversing *Reefseeker*'s aft deck. The score sheets, a calculator and razor-sharp filleting knives were neatly laid out on an old plastic table nearby and more than a dozen large ice-filled eskies were ready to take receipt of what was expected to be a record catch.

Occasionally a diver would swim in, heave themselves, their speargun and their fish aboard. Those who know him well say Merv can calculate the weight and points value for a fish without the need for scales, calculators or tables. Over the years he has weighed in so many fish he just knows. Before the diver placed their fish on the scales he had mentally, almost unconsciously, calculated its worth. Parrot fish, 2 kilos, 120 points; coral trout, 3.7 kilos, 137 points. And so it went on. As the scores were announced Merv would nod his head then turn his attention to the next fish. It was a game, a way of seeing how the competition was progressing, what fish were around. It would keep him amused until sign-off.

When *Reefseeker* first laid anchor at around 6.30 am, it had good protection from the easterly swell, and on a calm sea, the gap between Merv's mental calculation and the announcement of the scores was a matter of seconds. But as the morning progressed the sea shifted around to the south-east. In seafaring terms it would be described as a mild swell, nothing to get excited about, but it was enough to unsettle the scales. Over the course of the morning the interval between Merv's instant calculation and the official announcement steadily increased. By 10.30 am, the needle on the old spring-balanced scales was bouncing like a bungee chord and Mike called it quits. The four men packed up the scales, the score sheets and calculator, then commandeered *Reefseeker*'s runabout and an esky packed with cool drinks.

Merv put on a wide-brimmed canvas hat and daubed his face and the back of his hands with zinc. Tropical sun was no friend to an Irish skin, as he well knew. He picked up his jacket and climbed into the runabout alongside Greg Dockar. Greg gave the ripcord a swift yank and the little outboard puttered into action.

As the boat motored over to Erskine Island Merv, like everyone else, was convinced things were running smoothly. Shifting the weigh-in to Erskine didn't seem like a big deal at the time. All they would have to do was ferry the catches over to *Reefseeker* every half hour or so and have the fish placed on ice — nothing to it.

Two months later Merv wrote, 'I am sure that had we still been aboard the *Reefseeker* we would have noticed the possible danger earlier'.

He was referring to the cues of a dangerous current: the increasing drag on the lines hanging off *Reefseeker*'s stern, the eddy building off the vessel's twin hulls. He would have seen them all and had time to act.

Merv would also have seen danger from another, unexpected source: *Reefseeker*'s two deckhands were filleting the fish as they were brought aboard, then hurling the guts and skeletons over the side. Merv would have seen the carcasses streaming away with the current. He would have seen the sharks starting to circle under the boat.

Blabster had his path mapped out from the moment *Reefseeker* set out in the darkness. He woke before dawn, made coffee in the galley, then climbed the stairs to her upper deck. As the boat chugged the final few kilometres towards the island he watched the sky and sea turn from ink black, to steel grey, to a shade of blue not seen in the cities. He watched the shearwaters swoop and reel across the waves and for a while he sipped on his coffee, savoured the serenity and reminisced about his years of spearfishing in the Coral Sea.

From his vantage point one storey above the waves, he could judge the depth of water from the shade of blue. He could make out the shoals and bomboras a few metres below the surface. From the shape of the reef and the colour of the water he could tell how the currents moved around the reef. To the quietly spoken man with a drooping moustache it was like reading a street directory.

Blabster didn't have any aspirations of winning the 1983 championships but he was confident his knowledge of the reef and its fish would stand him in good stead. Even so, he planned for trouble.

'From the start I knew it was going to be a huge tide. I also knew I wasn't strong enough to swim against it. I would have to turn back very early if I wasn't to get caught out.'

When the competition got under way he sprinted across Erskine and swam out hard. As he told young Vlado and the other boys, competitive spearfishing was all about knowing what to look for and getting there first.

'I always look for the corner of the reef near a channel', he said. 'That's where the baitfish congregate and the currents bring schooling fish in close.'

In his experience fish were more flighty and powerful up north. They knew what a speargun was and what it could do. For those reasons, he preferred to fish alone. But he remembers one person fishing close by.

It was about an hour into the comp when I felt the current picking up. At that stage it was still swimmable. I saw Sue Dockar's buoy a short distance away so shouted to her, 'The current's picking up, Sue. Time to head in'. She shouted back that she was OK, so I said I'd see her at the weigh-in and headed back. That would have been around 10.30.

By 10.30 am Sue Dockar had two fish on her rig. There was a black-tipped reef shark hanging around so she pulled her line in and tied her fish off close by. She knew there was no way a reef shark would take her on. But given half a chance it would take her fish and she had worked too hard for that to happen.

'Not long after Blabster left, I heard an outboard motor', recalls Sue.

> I looked up and saw one of the safety boats heading my way so I stopped fishing. The guy brought the boat alongside and said, 'The current's picking up, time to head in'. He asked me if I needed a lift.
>
> I remember feeling a current, but at that stage but it wasn't too bad. Anyway, if I'd accepted a lift I would have been disqualified. So I told him I was OK. Then he brought the boat around and took off.

Silent minutes pass.

'I still turn it over in my mind and think, "If only I'd headed in with him, none of this would have happened".'

SWEPT AWAY

That was my first exposure to a current where you have no control over what you are doing and the current dictates totally what you do.

Paul Welsby

Around 10.30 am the current around Erskine Island shifted gear. The AUF's official account indicates a tidal stream of 2 to 2.5 knots, the equivalent of walking pace. Those divers on the northern side of Erskine Island would have to swim 400 to 600 metres across and, in some instances, directly into the current. Just to remain stationary they would have to match its speed. To make headway they would have to swim in excess of that speed by at least half a knot.

To put this in some kind of perspective, in 2001 Grant Hackett swam 1500 metres in a world record 14 minutes 34.56 seconds — an average speed of 6.17 kilometres per hour, or 3.33 knots. This was, of course, in a purpose-built Olympic pool, by the fastest known swimmer over 1500 metres in the world, in an event for which he spent years preparing. After that 14 minutes and 34.56 seconds he climbed out of the pool triumphant but, by his own admission, physically and mentally exhausted. Swimming at

3.33 knots in a 2 knot current it would have taken Grant Hackett 15 minutes to cover 615 metres. In a 2.5 knot current he would not have made it to shore.

When the competition commenced Mark and Vlado raced across Erskine Island, out onto the northern sandspit and threw themselves into the sea. Then, 1200 kilometres from home and about to face the biggest challenge in their short lives, they went their separate ways.

Mark Colys had two things going for him. First, the fifteen-year-old did not subscribe to conventional wisdom. The scrawny teenager wearing a ragged hand-me-down wetsuit truly believed his natural hunting skills and hunger to win gave him a competitive edge over the favoured Queensland team. Second, he trusted his instincts. So Mark found himself in rather a quandary when, after fishing for only half an hour in his first national championships, something inside told him to turn back.

> I didn't want to. I was in a good spot with plenty of fish. There wasn't much of a current at that stage, but I turned back anyway. Shortly after that the current started to move. It wasn't a gradual thing either; one minute there was no current, next thing you know — WHAM! — I'm heading for Fiji!

For a while he thought he could beat it. After all, it wasn't far, a bit over 500 metres to shore. Back home he had often swum twice that distance, in cold, rough seas too. So he let his gun and his fish hang behind him and for the next half hour he swam overarm as hard as he could.

Going by previous experience, Mark reckoned half an hour's hard swim should have placed him around 200 metres from shore and out of the main current. That experience had taught him to tolerate the steadily increasing pain in his thighs and calves, to accept his rapid heart rate and the burning sensation in his lungs. It was par for the course in competition, par for the course if he wanted to win. But even he had to admit it he was doing it tough.

> I'd swum in currents but this was different. After half an hour I looked up and Erskine Island seemed to be as far away as it had been before. By then my legs were giving out and I could feel myself starting to panic so I stopped swimming for a moment and looked around for a safety boat. As soon as I did the current dragged me backwards. I put my speargun against my shoulder with the spear and shaft out of the water as a distress signal and made myself swim on. I was scared and totally exhausted but there was no choice other than to keep going.

When fatigue threatens and panic strikes, even the fittest, most rational person can lose perspective, become overwhelmed and drown. Mark was lucky. He still had sufficient self-control for logical thought, but even so he was rapidly running out of options. He swam hard, his dwindling energy focused on a shallow section of reef up ahead. All he had left was old Blabster's advice: 'If you get caught out, tie yourself off and rest'. He took a breath, dived down and wrapped his rigline around a large lump of coral.

> Once the line was fast I knew I didn't have to fight the current any more. As I came to the surface, the current hurled me backwards. It pulled my rigline taut in seconds. I just lay there for a while. I was absolutely buggered. Everything hurt, my arms, my legs, my lungs, but I didn't care. At least I wasn't going anywhere!
>
> I was getting mad though. I'd been in the water all this time and hadn't seen a safety boat once. What if I'd been hurt or really been in trouble? What then, eh? As it was, my legs were cramping badly and I knew that I couldn't keep swimming forever. And time was running out. At the rate I was going I

wouldn't make it in before sign-off and I'd be disqualified. I had to get going, so I dived down and released the rope.

By that stage a few sharks had started to hang around — reefies and a couple of bronzies — so I pulled my fish in close. All the books say when you're in trouble you ditch your gear, especially when you've got fish, especially when there's a pack of sharks circling you. I knew that I should let everything go, but I was young, inexperienced and my only concern was getting my fish back to the weigh-in. I'd come this far, I sure as hell wasn't going to ditch my gear after all this!

Instead of swimming into the current, I swam across it, tacking like a sailboat with my new mates following behind. Every so often I'd dive down and tie off again to give myself a rest; or as I got closer in, I'd dive down and drag myself along the bottom. The sharks followed me all the way in.

It took me well over two hours and every bit of energy and willpower I had to make it back to Erskine. When I finally got to shore, it was all I could do to haul myself out of the water. I had to sit on the beach for a while, my legs were so weak they were shaking and I couldn't stand up.

I looked back at the water with a mixture of exhaustion and relief. From the beach the sea looked so calm.

'When that whistle blew we just took off!' says Vlado.

I'm hanging onto two guns and floats and everything else people suggested I take with me 'just in case'. I looked like a one-man band.

All I can remember is running into this beautiful clear water, my heart's pumping and the first thing that happened was I got tangled up in my ropes. There I am tied up in this spaghetti and I look across and there on this beautiful white sand, was a big bronzie [bronze whaler shark] in about 3 feet of water —

crystal clear water. It just hung there, motionless. I can still picture it, even the sun on its back and the shadow on the sand. It was so magnificent but so scary at the same time.

I was desperately trying to untangle myself without taking my eyes off him. My heart was jumping out of me. I looked away just for a moment and when I looked back there was just sand. I kept looking around but couldn't see him so I headed out from the island and started to fish.

At first it wasn't too bad. I was just blown away by the colours of the reef and how clear the water was. Then the current started to move. It just got stronger and stronger. All I could do was put my head down and swim in as hard as I could.

The next thing I remember is this turtle came level with me. The current was really pumping by then and that turtle went past as if there was no current whatsoever. There I am trying to fight my way back to shore and I'm overtaken by a turtle! All the time I'm thinking, 'This is not right, this is not right. How did I ever get in the NSW team? I'm not up to this!'

Alone and in trouble, Vlado Hric, with his two guns and his two rigs, with his heart pounding like a steam train, was desperate for a way out. Like Mark Colys, all he had left was Blabster's advice.

He spent the next two hours alternately tying off, tacking across the current and dragging himself, his fish and his gear along the bottom. Like Mark, when he finally reached the shore it was all he could do to crawl up the beach, sit on the sand and stare back at the sea. It did not even occur to Vlado that conditions on the day were extraordinary.

'Sharks, currents, I thought that was just the way things were in Queensland. I thought I'd just stuffed up.'

Shortly after Blabster left her, Sue checked her watch, looked across to Erskine Island and started to swim in. It was a little after

10.30 am. She stared down into the blue water, the grip of her gun resting in her right hand, the steel shaft trailing by her leg. She checked the shark on the edge of her vision and pulled her fish a little closer.

I would have been around 500 maybe 600 metres out. There was a cross-current but I was making headway. I certainly had no qualms about swimming back to Erskine. My main concern was picking up a few more fish along the way.

That's when it happened. In the space of what seemed like a few minutes the current picked up considerably. It was incredible — as if someone had flicked a power switch on. I just put my head down and pushed on. At that point I was convinced I could beat it. I'd swum in currents plenty of times and always made it back.

I swam for maybe fifteen minutes, sure that I'd make a bit of ground. It was quite a shock when I looked up and realized I'd hardly moved. I started swimming again. This time I tried to streamline myself a bit, conscious that I should keep my body as straight as possible and my gun in close. I was getting tired and my legs were starting to cramp but the only thing I could do was keep going.

This time I swam for another ten maybe fifteen minutes, telling myself, 'You can do it girl, keep kicking, you can do it'. But it didn't seem to matter how much effort I put in, I was not making ground. If anything I could feel myself being pushed eastward away from the island and into deeper water.

By that stage I was in a lot of pain but I kept trying to push through it. But the more I pushed, the more exhausted and frustrated I became. Eventually I reached a point where I realized the current was just too strong and I wasn't going to make it back. I remember looking down and I couldn't see the bottom any more — it was too late for me to dive down and tie off. So I stopped swimming, dropped my weight belt and raised my gun above my head. The moment I stopped the current just picked me up and swept me away.

I can't remember feeling any strong emotion or fear as such. The current was incredible and the only practical option I had was to go with it. At that stage I had complete confidence the safety boats would pick me up. I just kept my eyes on *Reefseeker* and Erskine Island and my gun above my head. I knew I'd done everything right, everything by the book, but I still hated giving in.

Then I looked at my watch. It was a little after 11.00. I could see the boat but with the comp going on and so many people in the water I doubted anyone would even notice I was missing until sign-off. At the rate I was moving I would be miles away by then.

Around twelve o'clock, Andy Ruddock crawled up the beach, pulled his speargun and rig clear of the water then fell back onto the sand. Blood seeped from coral cuts on his hands and knees, his legs were cramping and he was breathing harder and faster than he cared to admit.

He had turned for land early, yet the current had swept him from the northern section of Erskine reef down to the far south-eastern edge. But he could read the sea and, when all was said and done, Andy Ruddock was as stubborn as a bad-tempered goat.

He had focused on the northern tip of Erskine and for the next couple of hours swam diagonally across the current, dragging his fish and his rig behind him, swearing into his snorkel as he went.

The only way back was to get into the lee of the island on the shallows and then just swim in, then every so often stop and tie yourself onto the bombie or dive down and just pull yourself along the bottom. That's what I did. I had safety boats coming up to me when I was swimming back. They'd lean over and we'd have a yak. Each time they'd asked me if I wanted a lift in. But this was a national title. I told them I was doing just fine.

Finally safe on the island, Andy sat up and stared at his hands. He didn't feel crash hot, and moments like these he seriously considered giving up smoking. But still, he had eight fish on his rig and it was getting close to sign-off. He stood up, gathered up his gear and walked around to the western side of the island.

After much consideration, the weigh-in party had finally selected a patch of sand high up the beach. They set up a new station, carefully hanging the scales from a rusty tripod and placing their beach chairs facing the sea. Merv retrieved a few drinks from the esky and handed them around. For a while, they were content to watch *Reefseeker* nodding on her anchor chain and talk about fish and who was going to win the test match in the cricket.

Greg Dockar sat back in his chair and pushed his hat forward over his face. He let his eyes rest in the cool darkness and listened to the sound of the waves gently lapping on the beach. The early morning chaos had faded into memory. In his safe black space, order and boundaries were re-established, confidence restored — a state of affairs fortified by the gentle banter going on around him, but most of all by the reassuring presence of Merv Sheehan.

Around midday Greg Dockar was enjoying the feel of the sun's warmth through his T-shirt and the coolness of the drink can against his fingertips. He pushed his hat up to tell Merv he was looking forward to lunch. Then he saw the scrawny teenager in the ragged hand-me-down wetsuit approaching like a storm front.

Mark Colys had stopped feeling relieved. Pain, exhaustion, fear, anger swept back in and surged around in his brain. He was mad at the organizers of the competition for letting it go ahead. Mad at the safety boat crew for not seeing him in distress.

'Basically I was mad at everyone', he said.

> I grabbed my gear and staggered around to the other side of the island. There was Merv sitting back enjoying the sun and chatting to Greg Dockar. That was it. I went up to him and threw my gear at his feet. I told Merv he could stuff the competition: I wasn't going out there again. I could hear myself shouting at him, I was so angry. He told me to calm down and tell him what happened. I said I wasn't calming down. That current was fucking screaming through — didn't it bother anyone?
>
> Merv told me to take it easy. Take it easy!

Mark stood silent and stared back at Merv, his eyes wide and fists clenched. There were so many things he wanted to say, a whole mob of emotions clamouring for a target. But when he looked into the older man's eyes he found the words choked in his throat.

> Then I looked around at the other officials sitting there. They were smiling. They seemed to think it was all some kind of joke, you know, junior from interstate can't handle the conditions, yeah, big laugh. I had to walk away at that point. I'd had enough.

Mark Colys picked up his gear, turned his back and headed down the beach. There was a pause, then a snigger. Mark didn't want to look back at those stupid grinning faces. He just kept walking, the hot sand burning the bare soles of his feet.

> I walked around to the edge of the lagoon. There were a group of juniors sitting up the beach so I sat with them. I can't remember when Vlado came around but I remember sitting

with him and talking about the currents and the sharks. Both of us were pretty freaked out.

For a while they sat on the steep sandy beach hurling lumps of dead coral at the sea. It looked so calm, so inviting; fish swimming only metres from shore, shearwaters racing across flat blue water and out over the wide, white-crested rim of the lagoon. For the first time Mark and Vlado had been well and truly caught out by the sea. One young man was left questioning his own abilities, the other swearing he would never look to anyone for help again. Yet neither would admit defeat. For a while they licked their wounds and cursed the ignorance of the Queensland organizers. Then, gradually, bravado took hold. Hey, they'd fended off sharks, fought their way back to shore! What a story!

'Merv came over a bit later to see if we were OK', said Mark. 'He sat with us for a long time, listening to what we had to say. But by then it was all too late.'

CHAOS

I saw Scottie Smiles go past. He would have missed the boat by inches. He had his hand out and you could see the distress on his face. He just missed the rope.

Vlado Hric

From Keppel Bay just north of Gladstone the ebb tide flows relatively uninhibited until 57 kilometres seaward where it meets Polmaise Reef, then Masthead and Erskine Islands then Wistari Reef. In this region, two things happen. First, these formations funnel the tidal stream along a north-west/south-east trajectory. Second, water depth gradually reduces from around 30 metres to 24 metres in the narrow channels between Masthead and Erskine Islands and Wistari Reef before the sea floor drops back to 30 then to 75 metres on the outer edge of the Capricorn Group. That volume of water banked up west of the Capricorn Group is drawn through narrow channels and literally spat out the other side. It is a silent, incredible force. Sitting in a deckchair on a tiny speck of island in the midst of it all was an increasingly uneasy Greg Dockar.

At first, he had thought it was funny. There was Mark Colys, all kneecaps and ears, jumping up and down and screaming at Merv.

He was half expecting Merv to flatten the kid there and then. But those sentiments were short-lived.

> Mark and Sue had fished the same comps for the last two years. They'd dived some horrible seas and I'd never heard either of them complain. For Mark to flip I knew something was wrong.
>
> That's when I started to worry about Sue. I hadn't seen her all morning. The more I thought about it, the more anxious I became. It was OK when I was busy but as soon as I had nothing to do this bad feeling would come back. I found myself looking around for Sue, asking divers if they'd seen her.
>
> More and more people came in complaining about the currents and losing fish to sharks. Even the top divers were having trouble. One guy came over and held up what was left of his catch; a couple of fish heads with big teeth marks underneath. He said he had been trying to get back to shore when a big hammerhead steamed in and ripped his fish clean off his rig!
>
> I was hoping Sue had been picked up by one of the safety boats, or she'd swum straight back to *Reefseeker*. But all the time I had this nagging feeling something bad had happened.

It was 12.50 pm — half an hour to sign-off. He assured himself that in thirty minutes it would all be over and he'd find his wife safe and sound back on *Reefseeker*. In the meantime he tried to keep his mind on weighing in fish and his concerns to himself.

In 1983, Allan Moore was eighteen years old. He was a capable, fit and ambitious diver. Standing a little over 196 centimetres he also ranked as the tallest member of the Queensland spearfishing team. He had spent much of his childhood diving off the north Queensland coastal town of Mackay. Up there, big tides and attentive sharks were 'all part of the scenery'. So when he raced into the sea that morning he was confident he could handle whatever came his way. Within no time at all Allan realized he was way out of his league.

That current was unreal. I was looking at the bottom and finning along the top and it felt as if I should be flying through the water but the bottom was hardly moving. To get forward I'd put on a burst with my arms, then I'd get tired and slow down and fin for a while and then just freestyle again. It took me over one and a quarter hours to swim back.

After that I was wary of being swept out so I walked back along the beach and hopped back in, in a spot protected from the current. That's when I felt this tug on my line. I thought, 'Oh God, it's a Noah!' [rhyming slang — Noah's Ark — for shark]. I only had four fish on my rig. I just couldn't afford to lose any. So I pulled my line in to see how the shark was looking.

As I pulled in my rig I saw my buoy coming towards me then behind it was this big fin sticking out of the water. In the water I could see its head and behind it this triangular mountain of muscle. It was coming towards me not fast, just coming straight towards me very comfortably. I yelled out 'SHIIIIT!'

I seriously thought about giving the fish back, but I thought, 'No way! Aussie championships, I've got to push him off and keep my fish'. He swam up to me so I held up my gun. As he swam onto me he opened his mouth and I pushed him away with my gun. He shook his head a bit, backed off, sank down and swam around on the bottom three or four times and then slowly wandered off into the distance. I waited for a couple of minutes, slowly finning around, then I took a breath and dived down. There he was in the gloom. I saw him side on and bolted to the surface. I was desperately looking round, waiting, waiting for him but I never saw him again. I didn't catch any more fish.

Mark and Vlado were sitting on the beach contemplating their next move. In theory the hard work was done. They'd made it back to Erskine in one piece. *Reefseeker* was only 50 metres or so out from the rim of the lagoon. All they had to do now was swim out over the rim and let the tide carry them down to the boat — too easy. But neither Mark nor Vlado was keen to get back in the water.

'There had been a lot of talk about sharks', says Mark.

One bloke said a big hammerhead was cruising around, and to be careful on the way out. Under the circumstances, us juniors thought it might be a good idea to sit around for a while and see what happened. But one of the lady competitors decided to take a chance and try to swim back to the boat. We tried to talk her out of it but she'd made up her mind. Anyway, off she went. I reckon she got about 10 metres out to where the reef dropped away slightly before she suddenly turned and started swimming back fast with this enormous dorsal fin behind her. She literally ran out of the water with her dive fins still on and then started pulling her rigline in fast.

The hammerhead had grabbed her buoy and fish and was racing up and down the beach, tearing the fish off the line. We all came over to help the lady, who by now was being pulled back into the water. It was crazy, this shark charging up and down the beach with a big red buoy hanging out of its mouth and us trying to pull the fish away from it. Eventually we managed to drag the buoy and what was left of the fish free. The hammerhead went mad after that, swimming fast around the lagoon, grabbing people's buoys and throwing them clean out of the water. I've never seen anything like it.

Merv came over to see what all the fuss was about. He wasn't too impressed with the idea of having juniors and ladies in the water with such an aggressive shark. I can't say I was particularly looking forward to it either but we had to get back to the *Reefseeker* if we were to finish the competition. Merv told us to wait for things to calm down a bit. Then he organized us into a group, juniors around the outside, and a couple of the ladies and the fish in the middle.

It must have looked odd as we got in the water, two ladies and four skinny juniors, spearguns at the ready to protect ourselves and our fish, just waiting for this thing to charge at us from nowhere.

For his thirty-first birthday, Sue Dockar had presented Greg with a diver's watch. Greg had made a few cautious attempts at snorkelling and Sue was keen to encourage this new pastime. She ignored the state-of-the-art digital watches 'Guaranteed to 100 metres', opting instead for one she considered capable of withstanding the harsh realities of life on a diver's arm: a Citizen, with a large, luminescent face, surrounded by thick steel bezel, a sturdy black rubber wrist strap and a strong steel tang to hold the strap in place. She had wrapped the box carefully and placed it on the bedside table while Greg slept. In the morning she watched the smile on his face as he peeled away the paper and opened the present.

Greg's passion for diving soon waned but the watch stayed. He wore it most days, took it off at night and placed it on the bedside table. That morning, Greg had strapped it to Sue's wrist as he had before so many competitions. It was a practical token of love and good luck. Now Sue found herself constantly referring to the large analogue face and wishing away the time until sign-off and rescue.

I was being swept along at a frightening rate but I could still see Erskine and the upper deck of *Reefseeker*. That was reassuring. I thought if I could see the boat, well, that meant someone just might see me. Even though it was killing my arms I kept my gun raised above my head hoping the reflection from the steel might catch someone's eye.

Every time I looked at the watch I thought about Greg. I wondered where he was and whether he'd realized I was missing. Deep down I knew no one would know until the competition was over. That's when they would do the head count and check the sign-on sheets. I just had to keep my cool until then.

It was a bit after midday when I noticed two whalers hanging around. I can't tell you how big they were, just that one was bigger than me. At first they kept a bit of distance but as time went on they got bolder and started to circle underneath me. I didn't want to give up my catch but I was in enough trouble as it was so I pulled my fish off the rig and threw them as far away from me as I could. The larger shark came to the surface briefly then both of them took off after my fish. I didn't watch them eat the fish — that's one thing you don't want to see when you're floating around the ocean on your own. I just watched them go, hoping it would be the last I saw of them.

When I was sure they were gone I raised my gun above my head again. I looked back to *Reefseeker* and boy I got a fright. In the time I'd been watching the sharks I'd been carried way out to the south-east of the island.

I remember this heavy feeling. I realized I was in a serious situation and I had to stay completely focused and in control. I kept telling myself, 'Stay calm, just stay calm, someone will come and pick you up soon'.

Ralph Whalley dragged himself up onto a shallow coral ledge, took off his mask and fins and waded up onto the beach. He was, to put it mildly, pissed off. He'd warned them Erskine was too exposed. Now look at it, boats screaming around pulling people out of the water, shark fins all over the place.

'It was an absolute bloody disaster', he says.

But at that moment anger was pointless. There were fourteen fish on his rig and half an hour to sign-off. His priority was getting back to *Reefseeker*. He ran over to the south-western side of Erskine and dived back into the sea.

Ray Inkpen was mindful of his duties. He had to be around 'just in case' someone needed him and he definitely had to be on deck for sign-off. So he limited his dive time to one hour and kept close to *Reefseeker*. But as Sue pointed out, 'The sea grants no favours'. Competition convenor or not, when the current picked up he found himself being silently dragged away like everyone else.

> It took me over half an hour swimming hard overarm to get back. When I did get there, all I could do was grab the duckboard and hold on. I just hung there for a while, absolutely rooted. I was told later there were sharks around the back of the boat, a couple of tigers and a large hammerhead. Apparently someone had been cleaning the fish at the back of the *Reefseeker*, which was bringing them in from everywhere. I didn't see any but you can often be in the water with sharks and not know it.

He can't remember how long he was there for, or who, if anyone, helped him aboard. Just that when he finally stood up the gravity of the situation slammed home.

> People were coming in exhausted. We were throwing lines to them and hauling them in. Blokes caught behind the boat were swimming overarm flat out and going nowhere. You've got to remember these guys were fit and used to doing it tough. But this current was something else. I remember one of the Western Australians was pinned over the anchor chain and couldn't move. In the end it took two blokes to help him off.

Ray knew he had a bad situation on his hands. He needed advice and he needed it fast. But Mike McDade and the rest of the officials were still on shore, and Ralph Whalley, Tim Paulsen and Ray Oakey, on whom he had relied for so long, were still in the water. Ray was on his own.

Really there was little he could do. There was no magic button he could press to call the event off. And although divers were being picked up by the boatload, it was not like a ship sinking or a freak wave engulfing a beach. There, people are desperate for rescue. These people were desperate to win. A handful had made it back to *Reefseeker*. The rest would fight to get back to the boat right up until the very last minute. Even if he could have called the event off and somehow managed to simultaneously pluck every single diver from the water the backlash would have been merciless.

So twenty-three-year-old Ray Inkpen, in charge of the 1983 Australian Underwater Championships, made the only decision that seemed possible — finish the competition. He grabbed the sign-off sheets and started taking down names as people were hauled aboard.

Fears of a shark attack evaporated as the tight huddle of juniors and ladies swam into the current and suddenly found themselves flying down the side of *Reefseeker*. Ahead they could see the mermaid lines streaming across the surface of the water like kites in a gale. Divers were clinging to them, white-crested bow waves extending off their bodies.

'The current by this stage must have been around 3 knots', said Mark.

As we came down the side of the boat, all of us knew that if we missed the ropes out off the stern, we wouldn't be able to swim against the current back to the boat. It turned out there was only one rope on the side we came down, so basically if you missed it, well that was it. Five of us were lucky. A couple grabbed a line hanging off the back of the boat, the rest of us just grabbed who or whatever we could and held on. I'd missed the rope but managed to grab someone's hand and clung onto it. One junior missed the rope and just got swept away. Someone was talking about sharks but by then I had no energy to worry about them. All I wanted to do was get back on the boat.

Once again Mark and Vlado found themselves dangling from a piece of rope with current racing around them. At least this time *Reefseeker*, and the end of their ordeal, was only metres away. But they would have to wait their turn. Ahead of them grown men were dragging themselves fist over fist up the line to get to her stern. Others just clung on, too exhausted to move. For the moment all they could do was hold on tight.

Andy Ruddock decided to sit on the beach and watch the sea before attempting to return to *Reefseeker*. After a while he spotted an eddy at the western tip of Erskine. That would give him enough shelter to swim out into the current and be carried straight to the boat. He swivelled his mask around from the back of his head to his face, pulled on his fins and headed out. He paddled over the shallow corals watching the sea-floor slope away beneath him. He kept paddling until he felt the current pushing along the right side of his body. Then he stopped, pulled his gear in close and let the sea do the rest. If it wasn't so serious it could have been a lot of fun.

'There was a line out the back of the boat with a little dinghy on it and people were yelling: "Grab the boat! Grab the boat!"', said Andy.

I was OK because I kept right in tight down the side of *Reefseeker* and was able to grab a line quite easily. But a lot of people sat off from the hull. When they tried to get in they couldn't because of the turbulence off her stern. They just got washed away.

When I finally got onboard the view from the back deck was mayhem. People were just screaming past. We were yelling out to people on the island to swim from further up-current but they couldn't hear us and were just jumping in opposite the boat, swimming out and getting carted away by the current. The safety boats were picking a lot of these people up and dropping them off near *Reefseeker*. Even then they couldn't get back to the boat and they'd be washed away and picked up again.

I ended up having to jump back in the water a few times to unhook riglines and help people onboard. There was a young girl, the safety boats dropped her off and she got caught up in her rig cord. It was all around the boat. She couldn't get through and then she got tangled in the bloody mermaid line. I ended up jumping in and grabbing her gun because it had got hooked around her leg. She couldn't turn back to unhook it off her legs because she was hanging on the rope and flapping that much. Nearly friggin' drowned herself off the back of the boat.

Despite the chaos, the currents, even the very real threat of shark attack, there were no reports of panic about the conditions.

'I don't think there was any panic, because people had full confidence in the safety boats', says Andy. 'The only people panicking were those who knew they weren't going to make it back in time.'

And there were plenty in that category. As Ralph had attempted to point out before the competition, *Reefseeker* was moored at the head of a shallow channel where the current was at its strongest. By 1 pm, the current was estimated at between 2.5 and 3 knots. Some fifteen divers were down-current of

Reefseeker's lines, desperately trying to claw their way back to the boat. As one man put it, they may as well have tried to swim up a waterfall.

Among those caught were two of Sue's team mates, Gunther Pfrengle and Paul Welsby.

'That current was something else', says Gunther.

> I was within a hundred metres of *Reefseeker* swimming flat out but going nowhere. I couldn't understand it. I thought I must have stuffed up, maybe I'd gone out too far or something, because that just shouldn't have happened. At the time I was extremely fit. A few days before the spearfishing comp, I'd broken the Australian 50 metre record in the finswimming championship preliminaries. But for all that, I couldn't make it back to *Reefseeker*.
>
> After a while I could only swim in five-minute bursts. Then I'd have to dive down and anchor myself to the bottom by my rigline so that I could rest and get my strength back. Each time I would only gain about 3 or 4 metres. The current was slowly wearing me down and as time went on I was forced to stop and tie myself off more often. In the end I admitted defeat and after fighting the current for over an hour, I tied myself off and waited for one of the safety boats to come around.

'The closer I got to *Reefseeker* the harder it got', says Paul Welsby.

> At a guess I spent half an hour trying desperately to get to the back of the boat but was unable to do so. I went from 50 to 40 to 30 to 50 metres behind the boat swimming as hard as I could overarm.
>
> I wasn't too worried. I remember there was quite a concentration of divers and floats behind *Reefseeker*. The safety boats were just sitting there watching us at that stage, waiting to pick us up.

In the dying minutes of the competition, Andy Ruddock joined one of the safety boat crews monitoring the pack of divers behind the lines. He remembers helping people out of the water and taking them back to *Reefseeker*. He remembers seeing Gunther and Paul swimming flat out and going nowhere. What really stuck in his mind however was the moment he finally spotted his mate Ralph Whalley.

> The three of them, Gunther, Paul and Ralph, were freestyling flat out behind the boat. Ralph didn't stick to his plan. Turned out he started in the same area as me out to the north-west. But there was an area out to the north-east he wanted to dive. That was fine but he left his run home too late.
>
> We came alongside and I remember the skipper leaning over the side of the boat and saying, 'Well do you want to get in? You're not going to make it back'. Can't remember exactly what Ralph said back but it wasn't very nice.

At precisely 1.20 pm, Ray Inkpen called 'time' on the first heat of the 1983 Australian Spearfishing Championships. Debate still rages as to precisely how many of the seventy-five divers made it back to the boat unaided and in time. Ray put the number at eighteen. Thirty-five divers were picked up due to exhaustion; the rest were still in the water.

Among those who made it were the two skinny juniors Mark Colys and Vlado Hric, their mentor Keith Brabham and the hard-drinking, heavy-smoking, more than a little overweight Andy Ruddock. Among those who didn't were some of the fittest, most experienced divers in Australia. Years later, asked if they would still have competed had they known just how bad things were going to be, the resounding answer was: 'Yes, but I'd dive it differently'.

As Gunther Pfrengle says, without a flicker of doubt, 'Sure I would. But next time I'd use the currents instead of fighting them'.

MISSING

From the minute Sue went missing, we had a job to do and that was all that mattered. All Sue had to do was stay alive. All we had to do was find her.

Ralph Whalley

In 1974, Bill Silvester published *The Down-under Scuba Diver*, a simple yet amazingly comprehensive diving manual. It provided straightforward instruction on the physics and physiology of diving, dive techniques and equipment, as well as advice on dive locations, marine life and underwater photography. In a time when most instructors were themselves self-taught and dive gear was predominantly made in the garage or gleaned from army disposal stores, his book swiftly assumed the status of bible. On the subject of currents he wrote:

> Where it is impossible to make headway against the current, do not doggedly swim into it. Move in a sideways direction across the force. Certainly you may end up ashore some distance from the point of entry, but it is better than not being able to reach safety at all.

And, if all else fails … 'Stay calm, inflate your buoyancy vest, ditch your weight belt, and float with the current'.

Silvester's advice still stands but it is now backed up by a whole swag of equipment and technology. Whistles, mirrors, safety sausages, surface marker buoys, dyes, EPIRBS, underwater flares, flashlights and strobes are but a few of the devices a diver might retrieve from their state-of-the-art buoyancy compensator should they find themselves in dire straits. Some even carry rations in watertight containers 'just in case'. If Sue had been carrying just one of these devices — just one — doubtless she would have been found within hours, if not minutes, of the alarm being raised.

But in the thirty-three years since Silvester wrote his book, in all the dive courses, textbooks, rescue and survival guides that have subsequently been written, one issue remains largely ignored: namely, that once you have calmly dropped your weight belt, inflated your buoyancy vest (if you have one) and signalled for help, you are, for all intents and purposes, on your own. That, while safety sausages, flares and EPIRBS are very good and they save lives, when all is said and done, what happens next is down to you and the little voice emanating from somewhere deep inside your brain.

By 1.20 pm *Reefseeker* and Erskine Island had disappeared from view. Sue's world consisted purely of sea and sky. She had no idea how far she had travelled nor did she really want to think about it, which was probably a good thing in the circumstances. With the current running at between 2.5 and 3 knots, it is estimated that by 1.20 pm she would have travelled around 10, maybe 12 kilometres. Even if things ran smoothly back at *Reefseeker*, by the time the search was under way she would travel another 4, maybe 5 kilometres. But for Sue, all that registered was the vast empty seascape stretching in every direction.

People keep asking if I was frightened. The straight answer is no. I had a situation and I was dealing with it as best I could. The main thing I felt was an incredible sense of guilt and frustration for getting caught out like that. I was annoyed with myself and worried people would think I was silly for getting lost. I knew they would have to launch a search and all I could think about was the inconvenience, drama and stress that would cause. I felt anxious and uneasy because I was put in a situation where I was the centre of attention. It is not something I'm used to or comfortable with. Everything else was secondary to those feelings because I knew I was OK and that I could cope.

She gave a shy laugh as if she was worried her answer was inadequate or might offend. Then conversation moved to safer ground.

By then I was in a fair bit of pain from constantly holding my gun above my head. My fins had started to chafe on my ankles and I could feel the wetsuit was cutting into the back of my legs. At the time I thought, 'It's not that bad and there's nothing I can do anyway, so don't worry about it'.

Two decades after her ordeal she takes off her shoes and rolls up her shorts. Deep scars lace her ankles and the backs of her knees — ugly, jagged scars, silent testament to prolonged exertion and extreme pain.

'That was two days in the water twenty years ago', she says.

Sue had a strange luxury in her crisis — she was alone. There was no one to question her strategies, her motives or her competence. No one to pacify, worry about or reassure.

Ray Inkpen had no such luxury. 'It was absolute bedlam after the comp', he says.

By then most of the divers were somewhere in the vicinity of *Reefseeker*, if not aboard then in the safety boats or on the duckboard. A few were still in the water.

Part of my job was to say who was disqualified and who wasn't. Basically, if they were on the boat they were fine. If they weren't, well, that was the end of the comp for them. As you can imagine, this being a National Titles, there were a few people who weren't too happy about seeing their team mates disqualified and there was a lot of protesting going on. With all the arguing it took forever to get people aboard which in turn delayed the head count. If they'd just let me get on with my job we would have been able to get that head count under way earlier and Sue might not have spent two days in the water.

But at 1.30 pm there was no such consideration. Those divers crowded on the duckboard and aft deck were consumed in their own very personal drama — their four-hour battle with the currents and the sharks, and now perhaps worst of all, the young Ray Inkpen, sunglasses on, clipboard in hand, telling them their efforts and agony had come to nought.

The scene was tense, heated even. One man describes watching as Ray stood his ground while a man twice his age and a good head and shoulders above him leaned down and spat abuse into his face.

No one knew Sue was missing. No one knew that for every minute they argued Sue Dockar was being swept further away. At that precise moment their world was a spearfishing competition and their worth was measured in the buckets of dead fish on *Reefseeker*'s deck.

The weigh-in party packed up the scales and tally sheets and took one last walk around Erskine Island. Merv carried a garbage bag and as they walked Greg picked up discarded drink cans and bottles and dropped them in the bag.

'I remember Merv was saying it was highly disrespectful leaving litter in a national park and how he was going to have to talk to a few people when we got back to the boat', says Greg.

As he was talking I looked over and saw this bloke bringing Ralph's boat alongside *Reefseeker*. I gave Merv and Hendo a nudge because it was clear this guy didn't know how to drive the boat. I knew he was going to hit and BANG, he hit!

A bit later Ralph and *Reefseeker*'s skipper Doug came over in their boats to pick us up. Ralph was really pissed off. We could all see the ding on the side of his boat but none of us were game to bring it up. Anyway, Merv and Mike ended up travelling back with Ralph. I went in the rubber duck with Hendo and Doug.

As we came close to *Reefseeker* the current must have been running at close to 3 knots. I remember people crowded on the duckboard waiting to get inboard and this guy in the water clinging to a line. The force of the current was dragging his bathers off. There's a photo of him somewhere. It looks really funny, this guy clinging on for dear life and his bathers halfway down his legs, but it wasn't funny at the time. And the turbulence behind the boat! The safety crews were trying to come alongside *Reefseeker* and drop people off but the swell was short and sharp and it was hitting the hull side-on. The stern was flying up and slamming back down and there were people just hanging on. Basically, if you wanted to get aboard you had to make a leap for it.

I watched Ralph come alongside and Merv jump on. Then it was our turn. Just as we came alongside I looked down into the water and realized it was alive with sharks: whalers, tigers. I thought, 'Far out, there's no way I'm going to try and get aboard', because I knew with the stern jerking around I'd probably fall in and I could see what was waiting for me if I did. Looking back it was incredible no one was taken.

Then this fish carcass flew past my ear and I looked up and there's these two guys up on the fly deck gutting fish and hurling the guts into the sea. I don't know who they were or how they got on board but there they were, cigarettes hanging out of their mouths, totally oblivious to what was going on around them. It was as if they were on another planet. It was surreal. I yelled out, 'You bloody idiots! Can't you see what you're doing? Can't you see you're bringing the sharks in?'

Then I scanned the faces for Sue. It's weird how you can scan a whole bunch of people and know the person you're looking for isn't there. But that's how it was. At that moment, I knew she was gone.

Around 1.45 pm Ray announced that people were still unaccounted for. Protests and arguments were put aside as he called out the name of every person involved in the comp and the response, 'Here', boomeranged back. After fifteen minutes, two sign-off boxes remain stubbornly blank: Sue Dockar from New South Wales and Robert Morrison, a junior from South Australia.

'Sue Dockar and Robert Morrison', called Ray. 'Sue Dockar and Robert Morrison' — the names echoed around *Reefseeker*.

At 2 pm Sue Dockar and Robert Morrison were officially declared missing.

No one in their wildest dreams imagined Sue Dockar would spend one, let alone two nights at sea. It had never happened before. Come to think of it, it's never happened since — not to a spearo, not in a comp. So while Ray Inkpen and Merv Sheehan and a fair few others raced around trying to get a search under way, the majority of competitors were still more concerned about the outcome of the competition and the sharks hanging off the stern.

'It wasn't that people didn't care', says Gunther.

Most of us have got caught out by currents at some point and just about everyone was caught out that morning. I think people just assumed Sue and Bob would have tied off on the reef and waited for the safety boats to pick them up, so they didn't think too much more about it.

For me it was different. When I got into trouble Gerry Hill picked me up and brought me back to *Reefseeker*. He'd already retired from the comp because he couldn't get back in time. I was about to jump onboard *Reefseeker* when Merv shouted across that Sue and a junior from South Australia were missing. He asked me to go out and look for them. So that's what I did for the next couple of days.

Others took a dimmer view of their fellow competitors. 'I wasn't impressed', says Blabster. 'Not at all. Not with the way the comp turned out or the way some people behaved. There was a lot of animosity on that boat.'

Blabster was one of the few who made it back to *Reefseeker* before 1.20 pm. He was also one of the few who understood the danger Sue and Bob were in.

The most important thing in a situation like that is to get your facts right. Now, the last time I saw Sue was just before I turned back and she was out to the nor'east. There were good fish out there and she wanted to stay on. I turned back early and still had to fight my way back. I had to dive down and drag myself hand over hand across the reef, it was running so hard. All I knew was if she got taken from where I'd seen her she'd be miles away by two o'clock. Do you understand what I'm saying? Do you understand how far she would have travelled in that current?

I went straight over and told Merv where I'd seen Sue. But then one of the lady competitors piped up. I don't know who she was, but she was adamant she'd seen Sue on the island an hour later than I had. I thought, 'Fair enough' and didn't question it. Looking back, I should have because our whole search plan was based on what she'd said — and she was wrong.

Merv Sheehan wants to make one thing clear. He was not in charge of the search. He had no official role in the spearfishing championships apart from being NSW team manager. But somewhere around 2 pm it seems Merv assumed control on *Reefseeker*. Ray Inkpen may have been the convenor, Doug might have been skippering the boat, but it was Merv who demanded they radio for immediate assistance, Merv who ordered anyone not directly involved in the search to quit their bickering and act as lookouts along *Reefseeker*'s decks.

To Merv it wasn't about taking control. It was about getting people organized. About knowing what needed to be done and doing it fast so the safety crews could get on with the search. Sue Dockar was part of his team, she was a member of his spearfishing club, and Sue and Greg were his friends. And as for Bob Morrison, he was a junior. You just don't go around losing juniors! A few months later he wrote down his thoughts.

> Radio contact with Gladstone could not be made so a general radio call for assistance was made. Radio Brisbane answered and were advised of the urgency of the problem. They contacted Gladstone and direct radio contact was made with Gladstone ... We requested urgent air assistance for the search. The time was about 2.10 pm. We had to guarantee payment of air charter fees at $450 per hour for helicopters and $120 per hour for fixed wing aircraft before aircraft could be allocated. This guarantee was given and we were told an aircraft would arrive one and a half hours later.
>
> [Sue and Bob] were doing nearly 4 mph [around 7 kph] and we weren't sure what time the current caught them or in which

final direction they went. Thank God it was only a four-hour comp and not the usual six hours. This meant by 2 pm when we started, if they hadn't tied themselves to the sea-floor with their rig lines, they would have been miles away. With the *Reefseeker*'s speed of about 6–7 knots they would have already been out of our range.

Years later Merv remains highly critical of the response.

'We sent out an emergency call for assistance because two people's lives were at stake. How could they demand payment from us in a situation like that? Of course I guaranteed payment but I had no intention of paying.'

Ray Inkpen was also called to the bridge and asked to personally authorize costs.

Before they would send any aircraft I, in the capacity of competition convenor, had to give a personal guarantee that we would meet all costs. I was twenty-three years old and I just remember it as being a horrible, horrible position to be put in. Even now I would hate to see anyone put in that position.

At that point both Merv and Ray realized they, the spearos, were on their own. They looked across at the safety boats motoring around *Reefseeker*'s stern, to Gerry Hill and Don Norman, to John Powell and Rod Ashton, and finally to Ralph Whalley.

'No one knew the area or understood the currents better than Ralph did', says Merv.

From there on in, finding Sue and Bob would rest on his knowledge and his skill. If anyone was calling the shots it was Ralph.

Greg Dockar will never forget the moment Ray announced Sue and Bob were missing. He was sitting in a rubber duck with a large tiger shark cruising underneath him.

I can remember knowing what they were going to say before they said it. There was a feeling that you could cut. I felt cold and numb. Like it was a bad dream. Like any minute, I was going to turn around and I'd see Sue on the boat, or across on the island waving to us. But I didn't.

There was a lot of talking and shouting on *Reefseeker*. Merv and a few others were trying to organize a search and work out just when Sue and Bob had been taken by the current. The rest of them were watching the tiger shark hanging off the stern of *Reefseeker*. Ralph carried on swearing at the guy who bashed his boat up until Merv interrupted and started talking about where to search. I just wanted to get out there and find Sue so I thought, 'Bugger the sharks!' and jumped across to Ralph's boat. Next thing we're heading down-current.

There were five boats, about five men in each, with the boats fanned out into a line so we could cover the widest area possible. Ralph Whalley was driving our boat with his mate Tim Paulsen up the front and two other guys.

All I could think of was finding Sue. I tried to look at everything at once and ended up seeing nothing. I'd see a crest of a wave and think it was her. And the amount of bottles and oil drums we chased was nobody's business. The two other guys in the boat started to talk about what was going to be done with the fish caught during the competition. I just wanted them to shut up and look.

It wasn't long into the search when a message came over the radio that a boat from Masthead Island had offered to help. Ralph said OK and gave the guy an area to cover. We carried on for a while, but next thing we know, there's another call on the radio; the guy had run out of petrol and got washed up on a reef. You wouldn't read about it! Ralph started swearing again. So did Tim. Looking back on it, it was funny, but at the time it was tempting to just leave the guy there. We'd got enough on our plate without him.

We left the others and came back to find him washed up on Polmaise Reef. We couldn't run a line to the boat, so Tim jumped out and swam across with a rope. Then it started: we tried to pull him off and nothing was happening. Ralph couldn't work out why. Then the bloke told us he'd anchored on the reef. Ralph and Tim really blew a gasket this time. They started swearing at him like I'd never heard anyone swear. Like I say, looking back on it now it's funny, but at the time we could have ... Well, you know what I mean. We just wanted to find Sue and Bob.

Eventually we managed to tow him round to the lee side of Masthead and left him there to drift in. Ralph said something like, 'Bugger it, let's have something to eat', and pulled out some pears. We hadn't eaten since 4 am and we were all hungry. Ralph said we weren't going to be any good to anyone if we were thinking about food instead of searching.

This was the first chance I'd had to really look at Ralph and Tim. I mean, you don't go eyeing guys up at spearfishing competitions if you want to come away with your head on, particularly when they come as big as these two. Both of them were tall men, and broad as well. Tim especially, he was built like a bear and to me he had that look of someone you just wouldn't mess with.

We started to talk about where Sue and Bob might be. Ralph was pretty sure that wherever they were the current that took them out was going to bring them back. Tim agreed. I felt a lot better for that. It was the first constructive comment I'd heard all day.

Then one of the other guys asked who had won the competition. Him and the other guy seemed more concerned with what was going to happen to the fish and who was taking out the trophy than Sue or Bob. They asked Ralph what he thought. Ralph shouted that for all he cared they could throw the fish away. He was pretty pissed off.

As soon as we'd eaten we started getting the boat going again. Something was up with the starter motor. We were all swearing by this stage. Tim yanked the cover off the engine and used a spanner to engage it manually. It took a while, but eventually we were off again. Ralph gunned it this time.

It was about 4 pm and the sun was starting to go down. A call came over the radio to say a person had been sighted at Erskine Island and could we investigate. Ralph turned the boat around and headed that way. I was thinking, 'Oh God, I hope it's Sue. Please let it be Sue'. But as we came towards the island I knew it wasn't her. Even from a distance I could feel it, without being close enough to see who it was. We came closer and I could see Bob Morrison standing there on the edge of the reef. I was pleased we'd found him, but I really wanted it to be Sue.

Now I was starting to get worried. He looked scared, I mean really scared. We called out to him to swim to the boat, it was only about 30 feet [9 metres]. We couldn't get any closer because of the reef, but he just stood there staring at us all wide-eyed. We tried everything to get him to swim out but he wasn't budging. In the end Tim yelled, 'Listen mate, if you don't swim out we're going to fucking leave you here'. He meant it too. That's when Bob finally gave in. He didn't so much swim out, it was more like an attempt to walk on water. I threw out a line and he scrambled up it like someone was after him.

What really sticks in my mind is how tightly he grabbed onto my hand when he reached the boat. And the look in his eyes — that kid was terrified. We got him aboard and took off again. Bob didn't say a word. He just sat there in the back of the boat all hunched up. We were all quiet for a while.

It turned out that Bob had managed to tie himself to the reef when the current started to move, but for the last four hours he'd been circled by sharks until the tide went down enough for him to stand on the coral. All I could think of was Sue.

Gradually the sun started to set. Under any other circumstances, I would have enjoyed watching it, but then it was the last thing I wanted to see. We were still chasing up sightings from the spotter plane, going down-current, up-current — you name it, we did it. But we didn't find Sue. We were all tired and hungry and burned from the sun. Conversation had long since ceased.

The idea that Sue would be in the water after dark made me feel sick. I kept thinking about that big tiger shark under the boat, about the look on Bob's face. I tried to put it out of my mind, but I couldn't. Instead I could feel myself getting more and more uptight. It must have showed, because Ralph started talking all of a sudden. 'Don't worry mate, conditions aren't right for sharks. The sea's a bit choppy and there's too much cloud. They won't see her.' From anyone else I would have said, 'Bullshit', but this was Ralph talking, and if that's what he said, then that's the way it was.

It was well after dark when we went back to Masthead Island where *Reefseeker* was anchored up. Ralph told me to go aboard and get some sleep so I'd be fresh for the morning. I didn't argue. I was tired and confused. Ralph seemed to be the only person making any sense so I did what he said.

I could feel people staring at me. I just wanted them to go away. Merv came over and we spoke for a while. I could talk to Merv. I knew he was as worried for Sue as I was. Later, I decided to go up on the top deck so I could be alone and think.

I sat up there for God knows how long. It all seemed so different at night — the feel, even the smell of the sea had changed.

I can remember looking out at the waves and trying to think what it must be like for Sue all alone in the water. Then someone came up the stairs, saw me and went away. I realized that tears were streaming down my face and what I must have looked like, but I really didn't give a damn. I'd never cried openly before, but when I thought about Sue and how I'd watched her run off into the sea that morning I felt as if my heart was going to break.

She was lost and there was nothing I could do about it.

13

SEARCH

**When our back is against the wall none of us knows
what we are going to do. But I think you would
be surprised what the average person can do once
their back is against the wall.**

Paul Featherstone, OA, rescue paramedic, Special Casualty Access Team

It took several lonely hours for Sue to accept that 'loss of face' was the least of her worries. She had held her gun above her head the entire time, sure that at any moment the harsh drone of a boat engine would break the silence and the safety crew would come flying across the waves. The scenario was locked in her mind. She would be deeply embarrassed and apologise profusely, and no doubt there would be a fair bit of ribbing to endure back on *Reefseeker*, but at least her ordeal would be over. Tomorrow was the second day of competition. Who knows, if she worked hard and caught some good fish she might still be in the running.

But by six o'clock the grim reality of her circumstance had struck home. The safety crews were not coming, light was fading and her last chance of rescue rested with the pilot and observer of a spotter plane flying high above.

I'd seen the plane a few times that afternoon. Each time it came around I rolled back onto the water like a starfish trying to make myself as visible as possible. I kept thinking, 'Please let them see me'. But they never did. To be honest, I didn't think they would. I couldn't see the pilot so how could they see me?

The last time they came around I was really praying I was wrong because the sun was getting low and I knew once the sun went down the search would be called off and I was in the water for the night. I can tell you that was a frightening prospect. I just lay there watching the plane circle, willing them to look my way. But the plane finished its manoeuvre then turned west back towards the mainland. I felt pretty low at that point.

I remember it was a beautiful sunset. It was like this big movie screen in front of me that I was looking at but not part of, if you know what I mean. I was just hanging in the water watching the sky melt into these beautiful shades of crimson and gold and red. It was really peaceful. The sea was calm and there was no wind and there was no noise apart from the waves. It sounds crazy I know but there I was watching this magical sunset and thinking how wonderful it was. At the same time I knew I was facing a night in the open sea and my heart's racing and I'm telling myself, 'It's going to be OK. It's going to be OK. Just stay calm'.

After the sun went down everything went black, pitch black. I keep trying to think of something to compare it to, like being in a dark room or being lost in the bush, but there isn't anything. You're just floating in black and looking into black and knowing you just can't get out of it and you've got to deal with it. There's no sensation like it. I couldn't see what was beneath me or where the sea was taking me. At first I just hung in the water clinging to my float, telling myself, 'It's OK, it's OK', over and over again, in the hope that if I said it often enough I'd believe it.

Normally I don't think too much about sharks. I mean, you can't if you go spearfishing. It's sort of like driving — there are trucks on the road too. If one hit you it would probably crush your car and kill you. Every year people get killed like that but you don't spin out every time a truck comes past, do you? It's the same in spearfishing. You just accept sharks are there and get on with it. But that evening, sharks were most definitely on my mind. For the first hour or so I found myself waiting for a fin to break the surface or a nudge under the waves. There'd be a noise behind me and I'd swing around, bracing myself for an attack only to find there was nothing there but the sea. Every so often I'd peer down into the water, certain there was a shark beneath me just biding its time. But there was never anything there. It was just black.

I realized I was allowing my fears to get a grip on me, and brought myself back into line. I knew that my mind could create a far worse scenario than the one I was in and floating around in the dark I just couldn't allow that to happen. The only way I could deal with it was to keep telling myself sharks were out of my control. If one attacked I'd worry about it when it happened. I know that sounds really blasé but it wasn't. I was scared and it was my way of shutting them out. I still thought a lot about sharks. They never materialized, but I can't say they ever really left my thoughts. For a while I tried to put them out of my mind and think about dolphins; of the Flipper shows I'd seen as a child, where he rescues a person in trouble. Flipper never materialized either.

One time I looked down under the water and instead of the usual pitch black, I found my whole body was covered in a phosphorescent glow. Any movement I made created a flurry of luminous bubbles in the water. I'd never seen anything like it — these tiny particles of light floating in so much darkness. I moved my hand back and forth and watched the tiny bubbles of light appear and disappear into the black water. For a while

I stopped being afraid. I made little circles and big circles and figure of eights and watched the light trickle off my fingers. I was completely mesmerized by this magical lightshow. Then the light just vanished and I was left staring into a huge black void again.

It took a while but eventually I made myself swim on, hoping that I was only just out of sight of land. My compass had a luminous dial so even in the dark I felt I had a rough idea of where I was. I also knew the tide was probably running back in by now and if Ralph was right it would probably carry me back to Erskine later that night. I was pretty sure the current had carried me south-east which meant Masthead and Erskine must be off to the north-west. So I started swimming that way.

It was well after sunset when Ray Inkpen heard the boats returning. He hurried out of the main cabin, stepping over dive bags and buckets, around clusters of people. He reached the stern and watched as one by one the safety boats growled out of the night and into the harsh fluorescent glare of *Reefseeker*'s deck lights. Maybe the reports had been wrong. Maybe, just maybe, Sue had been picked up after the last radio message. But as his eyes darted from one person to the next all he saw were tired, expressionless faces burned by the sun and wind.

Ralph brought his boat alongside and dropped off Greg Dockar and Blabster. Greg stood on the duckboard, his hair and clothes drenched with sea spray. He looked stunned and confused. Blabster was gently telling him to step up onto the main deck but the words didn't seem to register. Greg just stood there. For the briefest moment he looked straight at Ray but it was as if Greg didn't even see him. Then Merv pushed his way through the crowd and put his hand on Greg's shoulder.

'Come on mate, let's get inside', he said.

Ray recalls that evening as one of the worst of his life.

By that stage I was really feeling out of my depth. I was too young and I hadn't got the local knowledge, the experience or the type of personality you need to handle a situation like that. Everybody seemed to want a piece of me. It didn't seem to register with anyone that I might be worried sick about Sue too, or that I was pissed off that the comp was stuffed up.

Reefseeker was anchored in the lee of Masthead Island, a safe distance from the island's skirting reef but close enough for her passengers to hear the mournful wails of mutton birds nesting high up on the beach. The search crews rafted their boats up alongside *Reefseeker* and climbed aboard. A small group of South Australians stood ready to embrace a clearly shaken Bob Morrison as he came over the gunwale. Most of the crew headed for the main cabin for something to eat or went down to the bunks for a shower and change of clothes. Ralph and Tim, still only wearing their speedos, went straight up to the wheelhouse.

Ray followed the two men up the stairs. He was painfully aware that by rights they should have been tucking into a barbecue by now and that the Ralph and Tim show would have been in full swing — a few pranks, probably at his expense, some tall tales — it would have all been part of the show. Instead, they crowded into the wheelhouse with Lennie, Doug and Merv and the only food on offer was a plate of stale sandwiches.

By then the immensity of their task was starting to hit home. Earlier in the evening a radio call had come through from the Australian Coastal Surveillance Centre in Canberra, otherwise known as Coastwatch. Gladstone Police had contacted them and asked them to prepare a search plan which was also provided to *Reefseeker*. The computer-generated plan took into account the east /west tidal stream, wind and drift. The plan suggested a 'probability area' of over 1850 square kilometres.

The men were tired and conversation was blunt. The skipper, Doug Walkden, spoke: some of the passengers were making an absolute pain in the arse of themselves. Either he took the boat back to Gladstone or they got off so he and his crew could concentrate on the search. Greg Dockar could stay. He was in no fit state to go anywhere. The South Australian boy, Morrison, he could stay aboard too, if he wanted to.

Ralph nodded. High tide was due around 11.30 pm. The safety crew could start ferrying people over to Masthead around 11 pm. There should be enough clearance to get the boats over the reef by then. After that, he suggested, *Reefseeker* should motor round and anchor behind Wistari Reef.

Doug offered the search crew bunks on *Reefseeker* for the night but Ralph said no. He believed the high tide would bring Sue back in that night and he wanted to do a couple of circuits of Erskine. If they didn't find her they'd tie up close by for the night and resume the search at dawn.

Merv suggested that if Sue wasn't found by first light they make up a dummy and drop it in the current around the time she went missing. 'We could wrap it in tinfoil, that way we can track it on radar', he said.

Ralph didn't think that would help — a deadweight would sit differently in the water to a person so it would travel a different course. Anyway, he knew where the currents had taken her — out behind Wistari — and they'd be bringing her back to Erskine again. 'She'll just keep going up, down, up, down, like a bloody yoyo.'

Doug disagreed. The tide could just as easily have taken her north-west as south-east. The only way of telling for sure was to place a dummy in the water around the time they believed Sue disappeared and track its movements. Ralph shook his head but when he looked around the room he saw that the decision had already been made.

'I just told them to get on with it', he says.

Half an hour later Ray Inkpen walked back down to the main deck. He called for quiet and made the announcement everyone knew was coming but no one wanted to hear: Sue Dockar was still missing. The competition was on hold until she was found. All those not directly involved in the search would be put off at Masthead Island on the high tide.

Ray knew it was a tough call but expected people to understand. To their credit, the majority did. There were plenty — including Bob Morrison — who volunteered to act as lookouts on the safety boats, plenty more who'd stood watch around *Reefseeker*'s decks right up to the moment when the sun met the sea. As for a day on the island, in the circumstances that was a small sacrifice. It might even be fun.

But a vocal few didn't see it that way. At the time Ray didn't know how to react. It had never occurred to him that anyone, particularly people he had long considered friends, could express such a callous disregard for human life. Years later, disbelief and disappointment still hang in his voice.

What made it worse was they were all my old mates. All they wanted to know was who had won that day's competition and what was going to happen to the fish. More to the point, what was going to happen to the second day of competition? When was it going to be held? That seemed to concern them more than the fact that Sue was still missing. This was a national competition and these people had come a long way to take part, but even so, I found their behaviour pretty nauseating.

I don't know if you've ever thought you could rely on someone and found out you couldn't but I can tell you it's not a good feeling. Then again, I suppose you get to see people for what they really are when the pressure's on, don't you?

Blabster was sitting in the main cabin when the announcement was made. He was not happy about going ashore, but he was 'too bloody tired to object'. So he sat back and sipped on his beer and let his mind wander through the events of that day.

I couldn't understand why we hadn't found her that afternoon, because by rights we should have. I was sitting there scratching my head trying to work out what had happened. Then I saw that girl come through the cabin, the one who said she'd seen Sue at around noon. I asked her if she was sure that was the time she'd seen her. She looked a bit embarrassed. Anyway, the long and the short of it was she hadn't seen Sue at all. It turned out she'd seen someone else and thought it was Sue.

I felt bloody awful because that meant if she'd gone from where I'd seen her then we hadn't gone anywhere near far enough down-current. We'd wasted that whole day.

Blabster got up and walked out to the main deck. He took a hand-rolled cigarette out of his tobacco tin and placed it to his lips. For a while he stood alone at the gunwale blowing plumes of smoke into the night. A soft breeze brought cool relief after the heavy, humid air of the day. He loved nights like these. He loved watching the stars and wondering where they came from and where they were going. He could sit for hours and look up at the stars. But that night all he could think of was Sue and what it would be like to float alone in that black water.

I kept thinking what I should have done and what I should have said. Sue was going to be in the water all night because I didn't challenge that woman. I can't tell you how bad I felt.

'I was tired but I didn't want to sleep just in case someone was out looking for me or the land was close by', says Sue.

Every so often I'd see a dark outline in the distance and, hoping it was an island, I'd start swimming towards it. Then a few moments later I'd look up again and realize all I'd seen were waves on the horizon. A few times that night I started to worry that I'd lost all sense of direction. I'd think, 'Maybe I'm just going round in circles or heading further out to sea and all this effort is useless'. At one point it all got a bit overwhelming and I had to stop and tell myself, 'Look, you're fit, you're buoyant and you know roughly where you're going. So far nothing has happened. You're doing OK'.

By then my whole body was aching. I could feel sores beginning to form on the sides of my mouth, and I knew my face and hands were sunburnt. I remember my neck and shoulders being very sore from holding up the gun during the day but I reckon it was my ankles that hurt the most. They were very swollen and rubbed raw by my fins. As the night wore on the pain became so intense that I had to take my fins off alternately and hang the free one off the spike on the middle of my buoy. Eventually even this wasn't enough, so I pulled out my dive knife and cut the sides of my fins for a bit of relief.

The pain made it hard to swim so I'd put my float under my chest and my arms out in front of me with my forearms resting over the shaft of my gun. It wasn't very elegant but it gave me a bit of relief and meant I could paddle along enough to keep me awake.

I thought about lots of things but nothing all at the same time. I was constantly looking at my watch thinking hours had passed but every time it was fifteen minutes, fifteen minutes. That was frustrating, as I really wanted the night to pass quickly.

I thought a lot about Greg. I kept wondering what he was doing and if he was OK. I thought about how awful I would feel if the tables were turned and he was lost and I was the one left to worry. I hoped Merv and the guys were looking after him. Then I started to wonder what he would do if I was never found. That thought played on my mind for a long time. It was something I'd never had to consider before. I'd always assumed we'd grow old together. I decided Greg would probably remarry, which annoyed me a little.

At one point the pain just got too much so I stopped swimming and I turned around and looked at the stars for a while. I remember tracing the outlines of the shapes I knew: the Southern Cross, the Bear, the Saucepan. The last time I'd really looked up at the stars was on a tour of the US. One night we were camping in Yellowstone National Park and I chose to sleep on the roof of our bus so I could lie back and look up at the stars.

A few times I pulled my buoy in close and tried to push up on it and scan the horizon. Everything was shades of black and inky black. There were no signs of life, just black waves as far as I could see so I'd put my head down again and swim on.

It must have been around midnight when I saw the lights — a small cluster of them a fair way off.

I thought maybe they were beacons or a lighthouse. To be quite honest I really didn't care, I just wanted to get there. I put my 'resting' fin on and started swimming again, heading for the closest, brightest light. My ankles were killing me by that stage but I wasn't giving up. I just slowed down, trying to pace myself for the distance.

As I got closer I realized they weren't beacons at all: the lights I was heading for were those of a large boat that I was sure was *Reefseeker*. From where I was, she appeared to be moored about 2 to 3 kilometres away. I stopped swimming and called out. With the sea being calm, I thought my voice must carry a long way over the water. I waited for a moment but there was no reply so I called out again and again. Nothing. There was no other choice but to swim for it. I let my buoy hang behind me and, ignoring the pain it caused my ankles, I swam as hard and fast as I could. I didn't care about sharks anymore. The only thing that mattered was getting back to the boat.

Merv Sheehan had no idea what precisely was bothering his friend. When he saw Blabster standing at the gunwale he assumed he was exhausted from the search and naturally concerned for Sue. So he went up to Blabster and for a while the two men stood together and stared into the night.

'We fucked up', said Blabster.

'I know.'

'No you don't Merv. No you don't.'

Merv turned and looked at his friend and Blabster's story poured out.

Merv was quiet for a long time.

'Shit', he said finally.

'Well, there's nothing we can do about it now.'

As Merv saw it they (himself and Blabster) had more pressing priorities. The first and most important was to find Sue. On that point, they both agreed with the decision to offload the passengers at Masthead. You simply couldn't have large numbers of people milling around interfering with the running of the ship when you were looking for somebody. And they would do everything they could to assist Ray in getting non-essential personnel off the boat.

The second priority, and to Merv's way of thinking a critical part of the first, was that they (Merv and Blabster) must stay on the boat. Certainly young Ray was doing a good job and he had the heart and that was the main thing. The problem was, he didn't have a great amount of experience. 'We, on the other hand, were both ex-navy. We knew that people who knew what they were doing were going to be required.'

But it was more than that and both men knew it. Blabster looked straight at Merv. He said, 'I'm not getting off this boat'. Merv said, 'Neither am I'.

For the next few hours, Merv and Blabster made sure provisions, cooking utensils and a first aid kit were packed and ready to go. They relayed Ray's instructions to the NSW team, organized the NSW juniors and pacified those reluctant to go ashore.

By 11.30 pm the majority of *Reefseeker*'s passengers were assembled in the main deck and cabin area. They had been told to travel light. Those well prepared took a sleeping bag, T-shirt, sunscreen, hat, sunglasses, a water bottle, towel, toothbrush and any supplies they'd managed to stash away. The rest had what they stood in. Spearguns and dive gear were banned. 'We've got enough on our plate with one missing diver, we don't want any more', were Ray's last words on the matter.

Merv took the opportunity to 'do an inspection' and 'make sure things were stowed properly and all of his team were accounted for'. He checked each of the bunkrooms for good measure then he came out and signalled to Blabster. 'I told Blabster to go and hide under one of the far bunks and not to come out until I told him to.'

Merv watched on as the safety crews unlashed their boats and came around to *Reefseeker*'s stern. Each boat picked up a small group of passengers and motored off towards the island. No one smiled, no one laughed, and those who'd complained earlier didn't let up.

Around 12.30 am the last few spearos climbed into *Reefseeker*'s runabout for the final trip over to Masthead. Ray Inkpen turned to Merv.

'It's time to go', he said.

But Merv remained where he was. 'I'm not going.'

'Come on Merv. Don't do this.'

'I said: I'm not going.'

And for a few moments no one spoke. Even the little group in the runabout sat quietly with their sleeping bags in their laps.

Merv had promised himself that he would not go too hard on young Ray. But he had made up his mind.

'Look Ray, you haven't got enough men here on the ship to put me off. I'm staying on. I think I've got some input I can give and I'm going to give it.'

'No you're not', said Ray as firmly as he could. 'I know you're upset. We all are, but you're going ashore!'

Merv remained where he was, his arms folded across his chest.

'Merv, I'm not going to ask you again.'

Merv didn't budge.

'Ray. This is only going to end up in a blue. I'm staying. And listen Blabster, you'd better come out from under that bloody bunk!'

There was a rustle from the sleeping cabin and moments later a sheepish looking Blabster walked out onto the main deck.

'Jesus bloody Christ!' shouted Ray.

Ray was exhausted and a hair's breadth from losing his cool. He looked around for support. Doug and his passengers looked back from the safety of the runabout. The two deckhands who'd been hanging around the stern had vanished. He turned back to face Merv. If he could have picked the stubborn old bastard up and thrown him over the side, chances are he would have. But when all was said and done, Ray knew that all Merv and Blabster wanted to do was help find Sue. To be left behind would tear them apart.

'I'm too buggered to argue any more', he said briskly and walked back to the main cabin.

And for once Merv Sheehan didn't say another word.

Reefseeker got under way sometime around 1 am. For a while Merv, Blabster and Ray remained on the main deck. Greg had gone upstairs — he wanted some time alone. In a way his absence was a relief because no matter how much they cared, no matter how much they wanted to find Sue and make things right, none of them quite knew what to say, or how to console him.

They were exhausted but it seemed wrong, somehow disloyal, to be comfortable or even to think of sleep. So they pushed stray dive bags and buckets back under the deck seats, retrieved odd pieces of food and rubbish, even tidied the main cabin. And when that was done they stood at the gunwale and stared into the night.

It didn't look good for Sue. No one wanted to say it out loud. So they talked about other things and made practical plans for watch rosters and thought about how they would look after Greg.

Eventually, Ray declared they were no use to anyone unless they got some rest so they said their good nights and went below.

'I couldn't sleep', says Merv. 'I went up to the top deck and all over the ocean you could hear these mutton birds wailing. It sounded just like a woman crying out in the night. The first time I heard it I thought it was Sue.'

On the main deck Blabster rested his elbows on the gunwale and blew smoke into the night. The clouds knitted together, blocking out the stars and soft drops of rain began to fall.

Somewhere out in the blackness Sue Dockar swam as hard and fast as she could. No one will ever know how close she came. All Sue knows is that every ounce of energy she had went into that swim and it felt like forever. Then, gradually, it dawned on her: *Reefseeker* was moving, albeit slowly, away from her.

I called after her in sheer desperation but there was no answer. *Reefseeker* kept true to her course and disappeared into the night. There was nothing I could do about it. All I could do was watch her go.

MASTHEAD ISLAND

Dawn and resurrection are synonymous.
The reappearance of the light is the same as
the survival of the soul.

Victor Hugo

Ralph Whalley was not a great fan of Easter or New Year and he tried his best to be way out of town when they came around. It was not the influx of tourists that irked him. It was the high tide, the alcohol and the inevitable knock on his door that came in the middle of the night.

'We were living up in Lucinda', says his wife, Anne. 'Every Easter there would be cars going in the river off the Herbert River Bridge. The young guys would get on the hooch in town and come home and speed across this bridge.'

'The old bridge was pulled down but all the pilings from the old bridge were still there', says Ralph. 'They'd go up and they'd lose it over the edge and what would happen is they'd hit a piling. Every time. They'd hit a piling and the doors would fly open and they'd wash out and we'd be up and down that frigging river in the middle of the night looking for people.'

'Every year', says Anne. 'If we were back from fishing the cops would come knocking and of course the river was in flood.'

Ralph has lost count of how many bodies he's fished out of the water. What he can tell you is this: a body full of alcohol floats to the surface in twenty-four hours, a body without takes three to four days; and some people — you can tell just by looking at them — they just gave up and drowned. Spearos don't do that. They fight.

It was 3 am. The five safety boats were anchored in the lee of Masthead Island. The sea was as black as the sky. The only noise came from the soft lapping of the waves on the hull and the gentle tink of empty beer cans rolling back and forth across the floor of Ralph's Shark Cat. Andy Ruddock was the first to crawl out of the tiny cabin, then Paul Riorden, Ralph Whalley and Timmy Paulsen.

Ralph fumbled in the dark for his packet of cigarettes and offered them around. It had not been a very pleasant night, what with the four of them jammed up in the nose of the boat, and Paulsen's snoring. On top of that his mind just wouldn't settle.

For the life of him, he could not work out why they hadn't found her the previous day. They'd followed the run of the tide, followed it way out past Wistari Reef. Not that you could really go wrong, mind you. All you had to do was follow the trail of fish guts they'd been throwing off the back of *Reefseeker*. It streamed down-current like a bloody paper trail and should have led them straight to her. But it hadn't. That meant one of two things: either she'd tied off and they'd missed her, which he doubted, or — more likely — they hadn't gone far enough.

Andy picked up one of the empty beer cans and tossed it into the boat rafted alongside them. Nothing happened so he threw another. As the third can flew across, John Powell's head appeared over the gunwale. Further along the reef a light flicked on on Don Norman's boat, then on Rod Ashton's and Gerry Hill's. There they were in their speedos and T-shirts, 60 kilometres seaward in the middle of the night: two fishermen, a sugar cane farmer, a dentist and a panel beater — five skippers and their volunteer crews to search more than 1800 square kilometres of ocean.

Paul Riorden opened a box of provisions from *Reefseeker* and found fruit, a few cans of baked beans and a loaf of bread. No one felt much like eating but it was going to be a long day so he slapped some baked bean sandwiches together and passed them around.

Gerry Hill's voice crackled over the radio.

'Ralph, you awake?'

'Course I'm bloody awake.'

'What's the plan?'

Ralph thought about this as he finished the last of his sandwich.

The tide would have brought her back in during the night, he said. If Sue hadn't made land or managed to tie off somewhere she'd be back out in 'the paddocks' behind Wistari by now. They'd start with a sweep around Masthead, then head over to Erskine, then move over towards Wistari.

Should they split up or stay together, asked Rod Ashton. Stick together, said Ralph. They'd run in parallel and maintain line of sight, that way they could comb each area thoroughly and move on.

At first light, the five boats formed up into a line and slowly motored around Masthead Island. There were clouds but it was calm and the wind was blowing at a pleasant 10 to 12 knots. It was enough, thought Ralph. Enough to keep a bit of chop on the surface and the bities on the bottom. As long as it stayed that way the sharks would leave Sue alone, he was sure of it.

No one in his boat talked about sharks, apart from young Riorden that was. He'd had a bit of a run-in with that tiger during the comp. A fair lump of a fish it was too, Paul reckoned. But the possibility that Sue might have been taken by a shark was never raised, not on Ralph's boat. In fact, in all the time Ralph searched for Sue he never thought she was dead.

'I don't know why but I never ever thought she was', he says.

There were three to five men in each craft, standing up, scanning the reef flat and grey waves for signs of life. They figured Sue would have ditched her weight belt, so she would be fairly buoyant, and if she had any sense she would have tied herself to her orange buoy. That would stand out quite clearly on the waves and also give her some support. But even then, little more than her head and shoulders would be clear of the water and the buoy was small, slightly bigger than a rugby ball. In short, they were searching for a bobbing head and a rugby ball in hundreds of kilometres of open sea.

Ralph knew it wasn't going to be easy. But between them they had decades of sea time. They had friendship and mutual respect. On top of that they had five fast boats and twenty pairs of eyes, a rough idea of where she'd be and a logical approach to searching the area. What goes out with the tide comes back in, Ralph told his search team over and over again. Sooner or later Sue would end up back at Erskine Island, he knew it. He just hoped she could keep her head until then.

The wedge-tailed shearwater is a dull brown, gull-sized seabird, with long, slim wings and, of course, a wedged tail. The name shearwater refers to the spectacular way it hugs the ocean in flight, using the updraft to gain altitude before turning gracefully on its side and skimming across the waves. From sun-up to sunset the birds stay far offshore, riding the winds, skimming the waves, hunting baitfish and squid. In the evening they congregate over the sea, hundreds of them swooping and reeling against the setting sun. But when they return to land the graceful spell is broken. Some say it's poor night vision, others that the birds' legs are set too far back on their bodies, making hopeless landing gear. But as daylight fades, the birds crash into trees, buildings, even unsuspecting tourists, and tumble to the ground. At that moment the elegant shearwater is transformed into a top-heavy, slightly comical creature that skitters off into the darkness.

From October to March approximately 1.5 million wedge-tailed shearwaters, along with half a million black noddies, 6000 crested and bridled terns, 10,000 black napped and 400 roseate terns descend on the island cays of the Capricorn Group. But while the terns and noddies roost in trees and bushes, the wedge-tailed shearwater uses its powerful legs to dig extensive, warren-like burrows. And while other birds court and breed in daylight hours, the wedge-tailed shearwater waits for nightfall, when courting couples sit on the ground and howl to each other for hours.

In the summer months their sorrowful calls pervade the coral cays, so much so that eighteenth century sailors assumed the cays were haunted. Only when shipwreck forced them ashore did they realize the ghostly wailing emanated from a seabird that also happened to be relatively large, meaty and easy to catch. And so it was that the wedge-tailed shearwater, so graceful in flight, so ungainly on land, became known as the mutton bird.

Of course little of this was known to the fifty or so spearos who waded onto shore and up the steep beach of Masthead Island in 1983. All they knew was that there were no lights apart from small hand-held torches. They had no map and no plan. All they could see was a thin strip of beach disappearing into a black wall of forest. All they could hear were the mournful calls of thousands of lovesick birds.

'At that stage there was a mix of emotions', recalls one member of the NSW team.

Bob Morrison had been found and it was just Sue that was overdue. While there was an underlying fear that she had gone, bravado took over. I don't think anyone really wanted to face the fact that she might be dead, so the sentiment went the other way. There were a few individuals actually blaming her for going missing. The actual sentiment being expressed that night was: 'Why is she putting us through this? Tomorrow she's going to be found and we'll have spent the night out here. We're hungry, tired and cold and, fuck, this is an inconvenience!'

But not everyone shared this view. Vlado, Mark, Scottie and Lennie stumbled along the beach, following the dancing torchlights and shadowy outlines of men up ahead. The night was cooler than they had expected and a light spit of rain started to fall shortly after they arrived. But it didn't seem to matter. Stars shone between the clouds and black silk waves gently caressed the beach. It was magical. Beautiful. Magnificent. All those words that teenage boys shrink from ever saying and instead funnel into one, all-encompassing descriptor.

'It was unreal!' says Mark, the excitement still ringing in his voice.

You've got to remember we were young kids at the time. We'd come up there for the comp and a holiday and all this happened. First the currents, then Sue, then we're dumped on this island in the middle of the night with just our sleeping bags.

'We were lucky', says Vlado. 'We didn't have to think of the consequences or the seriousness of the lost guys. For us it was all an adventure. "An Adventure." It was like Robinson Crusoe!'

The boys found a flat patch of scrub up close to the treeline and rolled out their sleeping bags. 'Things' were moving around their feet and there was a disconcerting crunching sensation as they walked. And the noise of the birds — it was enough to drive you mad. But there was nowhere else to go. So they sat in their little camp surrounded by creatures unknown and chewed the last of the lollies they'd 'borrowed' from service stations on the way up to Gladstone.

They didn't talk or even think about Sue. Not because they didn't care. Not because they didn't understand the danger she was in. In their world a comp was just a comp and death was something that happened to old people. Tomorrow the runabout would be back to pick them up and things would go back to normal. In the meantime they were castaways marooned on a desert island and they were determined to enjoy every moment.

Only in the soft light of dawn did the boys gain any real perspective on their situation. They sat up in theirs sleeping bags and looked out to sea. The tide was extraordinarily low, leaving the island's massive reef-flat little more than a vast shallow pool; and the narrow beach they stumbled along in the night had been transformed into a wide promenade of sand. But Vlado's most vivid memory was of their little camp in the scrub.

> We looked around us and that's when we realized what the crunching noise had been. The ground was alive with mutton bird nests. There was nowhere you could walk, they were so close to each other. After that we moved our gear down onto the sand.

It was a little after 5 am by the time they rose from their camp. They walked along the beach, past small clusters of tents and tarpaulins, past motionless bodies cocooned in sleeping bags and huddled under beach towels. They followed the gentle curve of sand around the island, playing games of tag and making barefoot sorties out onto the reef flat.

They continued on along the beach until half an hour later, they found themselves back at camp. By then most people were awake, either sitting in little groups on the sand or off on their own explorations. No one was quite sure what to do or who was in charge. There was, however, one thing they were agreed upon: they were hungry.

While Masthead Island is the second largest island in the Capricorn Group and the closest to the mainland, to this day it remains one of the most remote, undisturbed and botanically diverse coral cays in the southern section of the Great Barrier Reef. There is no fresh water, no toilets, no power. Queensland Parks and Wildlife

Service, which now manages the island, advises prospective campers they must be self-sufficient, right down to supplying their own dunny bucket and toilet seat. Back in 1983, apart from personal belongings, the fifty or so castaways had between them a day's supply of water, a large cooking pot, a few utensils, some pepper, three stock cubes and approximately 6 kilograms of frozen hamburger mince.

'They'd given us a whole heap of mincemeat and a pot', says Vlado. 'They just bundled it up, threw it in the boat and said, "We'll be back once we've found Sue". We had to virtually fend for ourselves.'

In normal circumstances this would not have presented a problem. They were, after all, skilled hunters in their ideal environment. But their guns were still on the boat and they had been ordered to stay out of the sea.

As the morning wore on, juniors from all the state teams gradually came together on the beach, not so much as a pack, more as a loose assortment of lost souls looking for something to do and, more importantly, something to eat. They would not go against the orders of the older divers, but in their book no one had said the reef flat was out of bounds. And there was nothing to say you needed a speargun to catch a fish.

'It was dead low tide', says Mark.

All us juniors took off out in the lagoons and started mustering up food. We were chasing all these tuskfish and parrot fishes right up under these ledges, sticking our arms in there and grabbing them by the throat and pulling them out.

Gradually, older divers joined in, picking their way across the reef, foraging in rock pools and shallow lagoons.

'I remember Les Gleeves', says Vlado.

He's a big quiet guy from our team, like a gentle giant. He waded out and clubbed a shark. It was a good size shark too! He looked like a caveman dragging it back up the beach. Then he made a big spear from a branch for us and we went after stingrays! He said, 'We'll slice them up, they're good tucker'.

By mid-morning the incoming tide was flooding back over the reef so the musterers returned to shore. NSW diver Peter Inskip somehow found himself in charge of the cooking pot and the catch. He called on a few juniors to collect driftwood but Mark managed to slip away.

Allan Moore had smuggled a facemask onto the island. Mark scrounged up another one and they set off to see what they could catch.

Only the day before, Allan and Mark had been eyeing each other off, as rivals do from the safety of their own team. Masthead had brought about an impromptu truce. As they walked along the beach they shared horror stories from the previous day — the currents, the hammerhead going crazy in the lagoon, the tiger shark under the boat. Then conversation turned to Sue.

'She's been gone all night', said Allan.

For once Mark, usually so slick with his responses, did not know what to say. Allan was smart enough to read the silence and let the matter drop. They stood and looked out at the ocean. Storm clouds hung over the island and balmy calm had descended on the sea. If they were to dive it had to be now. So they waded out into the water, put on their facemasks and swam out.

Their first conquest was a large squid. Mark used the light of his dive torch to coax it out from under a crevice and before it had time to react Allan had swept it up in a catchbag. A little while later they caught a second squid using the same technique. Then they saw long stick-like antenna protruding from under a ledge.

'We followed this ledge down, no fins, no gloves, no nothing and we ended up pulling out this 4 kilo painted cray', said Mark.

It was a female and when we turned it over it was full of eggs. Allan's going, 'You've got too let it go, let it go'. And I'm holding onto it thinking, 'I'm hungry and I don't care if it's full of eggs'. But Allan wouldn't let up and he was bigger than me so I put it back.

It was close to high tide when they returned to camp. By then the fire was lit and the first thin wafts of steam were rising from the cooking pot and a cricket match was in progress a little further along the beach. They handed in their catch and joined their friends watching the game. For a while Mark clapped and cheered as the balls flew across the beach.

There was still no word on Sue, no word on the search. Conversation shifted back to the previous day, to the currents, the catch, the sharks, the outcome of the competition, then to the inevitable: the chances of a woman surviving a night alone 'out there'.

'One of the worst things about that situation was we had no information', recalls one of the castaways. 'The shark stories started to play on our minds. Then the realization started to sink in: "Shit, she's probably gone".'

At first Mark was content just to watch the match and let the conversation pass. He was a junior. It was not his place to question his elders and betters. But then something snapped.

'People started grumbling because the comp had been cancelled', says Mark.

I actually even heard a few of them still wanting to hold the competition. I just couldn't believe it at the time. I turned around and said to them, 'You are talking about someone's life for chrissake!'

These were hardcore divers he had long revered. He knew spearfishing was an individual, not a team sport, and that mantle drew its share of loners. He also understood they had come a long way, further than most, spent a great deal of money and for what? But like Ray Inkpen he found himself incensed by their selfishness and cold-hearted indifference towards Sue.

'They didn't know her', he says flatly.

For Mark it was personal. He thought of the woman he knew, who never so much as raised her voice but punched into the elements with the best of them, the woman who never gave up.

> She might come across as a meek and mild lady but I'm telling you, I know Sue and she has the heart of a lion.

Sue Dockar heard the birds before she saw the dawn — black shapes darting overhead, calling to each other as they moved fast over the water. Then a soft yellow glow appeared on the horizon. She tried to lift her head off her buoy — an effort rewarded by a sharp shock of pain across her shoulders and up her neck. She let her head drop back down and a few moments later tried again. First she moved one arm, then the other, then braced herself and raised her head. As the pain shot through her back the sky rippled from grey, to red and gold; the sea turned from black, to silver, to blue. The sun slowly rose up out of the sea and suddenly the night was gone.

> I didn't feel much emotion at all. It was as if that part of me had closed off sometime during the night. I was certainly relieved the night was over and yes it felt good to see the sun come up. But I can't say I was taking in the beauty of the dawn or the way the light played on the waves. No way. All I could think about was that now I could see and be seen and ahead of me lay ten hours in which I could be rescued or make it back to an island.
>
> The first thing I did was take a full 360 degree scan. I was still out of sight of land with only a rough idea of where I was.
> re was no current but the movement of the sea was a bit

stronger than the day before and there were clouds on the horizon.

I just watched the sea, trying to work out where the swell was coming from in relation to the sunrise. The only thing I knew for sure was the sun rose in the east and it looked as if the swell was pushing me to the north-west to where I thought Erskine and Masthead were.

I started to swim with the swell. Well, not so much swim as lean across my buoy and paddle up and down the waves one fin on, the other off to relieve the pressure in my feet. My neck was killing me, and the swelling and sores on my legs and feet were getting worse. At that point I didn't know how bad things were. I just knew the skin behind my knees and around my ankles was getting chafed and it hurt a lot. But I also knew it was important to keep moving. It was more of a mental thing than any confidence in where I was going. Swimming kept my mind occupied and as long as I kept moving my mind stayed positive.

I wouldn't say I was convinced I was going to be found but I was fairly optimistic. Again it was a mental thing. I'd sort of made up my mind I wasn't going to die. People try to make out like that was brave and dramatic but it wasn't. It really wasn't. It was more like my little act of defiance. I kept thinking about Greg and how we had a home and how we'd planned to have kids and I wasn't going to let go of that buoy. No way.

I'm not saying I didn't get down or frightened. I don't know how other people deal with being lost at sea but I was constantly questioning myself. Even after the sun came up I found myself wondering if I was going the right way and how long it would be before the sharks took an interest in me. I'd have to stop and say to myself, 'Look, you survived the night, you're buoyant, the sharks haven't come for you, you're doing just fine, just hang in there'. I'd keep saying it and saying it until the bad thoughts went away. At the other extreme I'd be bored and think how slowly time was passing. To me that was just as dangerous as being negative because then I'd start thinking about all the things I couldn't control. That's why it was so important to keep swimming.

I wasn't moving terribly fast, mainly because the pain meant I constantly had to stop and swap my fin over to the other foot. So I'd swim for a while, stop, look around and then swim on. I saw a few helicopters but I realized they were probably just charter helicopters, as they kept roughly to the same route. A few got quite close though; directly overhead on a couple of occasions. Each time I saw one, it didn't matter how near or far, I'd lie flat on the waves, my gun in the air and my float and diver's flag as exposed as I could.

At first it was really uplifting but as the morning wore on I could feel myself getting more and more frustrated. It just didn't seem fair. I couldn't understand why they didn't see me, particularly when they were so close. I didn't cry and I didn't get angry or upset but it did start to pre-occupy me. I'd try telling myself how difficult it must be to spot a person in the water and that plenty more aircraft would fly over before the day was out, but I can't say it made me feel any better.

The big boost came when I started to catch little glimpses of green off in the distance. At first I though it was just the light playing tricks on me, as by then the clouds were directly overhead and the colours and shapes in the ocean had begun to change. Then a large wave came through and lifted me up and I saw it again. That time I was sure. They were a long way off but they were definitely trees. That was incredible. As soon as I saw them it was as if my whole situation changed. It proved I'd been right to trust my instincts. It was like I wasn't lost any more.

From the outline I figured it had to be Masthead Island and the trees were about 2 to 3 kilometres away. At the rate I was moving that meant I'd get there by mid-afternoon. I wanted to swim much harder but I knew I couldn't sustain such an effort for very long so I tried to maintain a steady pace.

I remember not long after that I stopped for a rest and looked up at the sky. I saw this big black cloud coming towards me with a grey sheet of rain underneath it. A few minutes later huge drops of rain began to fall. I started swimming and then, it seemed in a matter of seconds, this cloud was directly overhead and the rain was really pummelling the surface of the sea. I couldn't see Masthead any more. I couldn't even hear the sound of the waves. So I stopped swimming.

I wasn't thirsty. In fact I hadn't even thought about food or drink since I got swept away but I knew that while fresh water was around I should make the most of it. I was too frightened of losing my mask to take it off and use it as a cup so I put my head back and opened my mouth in an attempt to catch the rain drops as they fell. It must have looked very strange. There I was in the middle of the ocean, trying to catch raindrops in my mouth.

Greg Dockar opened his eyes and stared up at the base of the top bunk. He could hear people talking and was aware of pale light coming through the porthole. For a few moments his mind was blissfully numb. Then the nightmare flooded back and he scrambled out of bed.

The sun was starting to climb over the horizon when he rushed out onto the fly deck. In the half-light he could make out what appeared to be a wide, barren stretch of land extending far off into the distance and at first he thought they were anchored off an island. But as the sun climbed higher and the light began to change he realized it was low tide and the scene in front of him was not land at all but the jagged bedrock and exposed corals of Wistari Reef.

I was looking at the reef and it was well clear of the water and I was thinking maybe with the low tide Sue might be standing on some coral somewhere just waiting to be picked up like Bob Morrison was. I started looking around for the safety boats thinking, 'Come on guys, we've got to get moving before the tide comes back in', but I couldn't see the boats anywhere.

I could hear people moving around on the lower deck so I went downstairs. Merv was the first person I saw. I asked him where the safety boats were and he said they'd left before dawn. It took a few seconds for it to sink in but then I realized what he'd said: they'd left without me. They'd tricked me on to *Reefseeker* to get me out of the way.

Merv was trying to settle me down saying no, that wasn't the case at all. He said the boats had just anchored up behind Masthead and got going as soon as the sun had come up but I was furious. It was my wife out there. My wife! The only thing I could do for Sue was look and they'd taken even that away from me.

Greg became aware of other people in the main cabin: Blabster and Ray Johnson sitting at the table, bowls of cereal in their hands, Paul Welsby and Ray Inkpen at the doorway to the main deck. They were looking at him. It felt like they were all looking at him, but they didn't know what to say or what to do because when he looked back they looked away. It was not until much later that he found out his friends had taken turns on watch during the night; that Bob Morrison had taken his place in the search boats; that it was Doug who insisted Greg stay on *Reefseeker* where they could look after him. All Greg knew was that Sue was lost and so was he. He had never felt so lost and alone in his life.

'Merv told me to sit down and eat some breakfast', says Greg.

He said we were going to be under way in a few minutes and he wanted everyone on lookout duty.

I remember there was a lot of talk about where Sue could be. Merv and the skipper thought with the tide running like it was Sue could have gone way out past Wistari. I thought about how Ralph said the current would bring her back and that's what I said. In the end they decided we'd head east and work our way back to Erskine for the high tide.

We got under way a bit after 5.00 and I went up on the top deck. I can't remember who else was there, just that I was staring out over the sea and that with it being so high up you could see a long way.

I was still mad with the safety boat guys for going off without me. Looking back now I can understand it. I mean — they didn't know me, they didn't know how I'd react and if the tables were turned I probably would have done the same thing. I just wish someone had talked to me about it.

I was trying to stay calm and not think about sharks and stuff and I felt like I was handling the situation. I really believed Sue was alive. I mean, sharks only go for you if you're weak and I'd say to myself, 'My Soozy's not weak: she's fit and strong and she's a really good swimmer'.

And if you know Sue you know mentally she's as tough as any of the guys. But every so often things would get under my skin, like if I heard someone chatting I'd think, 'Just shut up and look!'

Merv was with me a lot of the time. He was pretty much calling the shots by then. I wouldn't say Merv was enjoying it at all but he was definitely in his element. He was telling everyone what to do.

One thing he did was constantly swap us around so we could rest our eyes because if you look too long at the same thing you look but you don't see — your mind switches off. Well, at one point he swapped us over and I looked at the horizon and saw these dirty great black clouds coming towards us. I thought, 'Christ, that's all Sue needs'.

A little while later the clouds came over us and it poured down but Merv and I, we stayed on deck. The rain didn't bother me and I don't think it bothered Merv because he was smiling. It was the first time I'd seen him smile since Sue went missing and him being happy raised my spirits too. He said, 'Water, Greg, fresh water! At least Sue's going to get a drink!'

THE LOWEST POINT

Courage is almost a contradiction in terms.
It means a strong desire to live taking the form of
a readiness to die.

GK Chesterton, Orthodoxy

From Erskine Island, the ebb tide sweeps around the southern edge of Wistari, past the lower extremities of Heron Island's fringing reef and on towards One Tree Island. Over that 33 kilometres, water depth steadily increases from 18 to 50 to 70 metres; the wave pattern shifts from the gentle swell afforded by the protection of the islands and reefs to the longer, heavier motion of the open ocean.

One Tree Island marks the outer edge of the Capricorn Group. The low shingle cay sits on the southern edge of a large lagoon. To those scientists who visit the island's modest research station, One Tree is 'an excellent example of the rich development characteristic of the southern part of the Great Barrier Reef'. But when Merv Sheehan looked across at the island from the deck of *Reefseeker* all he saw was the point of no return.

It was mid morning and the rain had come and gone, much like the smile on Merv's face. He could see ocean breakers crashing onto reef flats and charging at the channel between One Tree and Sykes Reef. He knew that within a few hundred metres the sea floor dropped away rapidly. There were no more shallow coral reefs, no islands to swim to. 'If she'd gone past One Tree that was it, she was gone.'

He started the day vowing to keep Greg as informed and involved in the search as he possibly could. But this was one concern he did not want to share so he went downstairs, poured a cup of coffee and walked out to the aft deck.

He didn't hear Blabster come out; he just became aware of the presence next to him and turned to see his friend. Blabster looked tired and drawn. The police launch was on its way out, he said. They should arrive at Erskine sometime around 3.00. Blabster started back up to the wheelhouse. Merv called after him.

'This isn't your fault', he said.

Reefseeker slowly motored north to Sykes Reef then turned back towards Heron Island. Merv noticed the cloud columns building and a slight stiffening in the breeze. Occasionally he saw a search plane or helicopter in the distance.

He thought about a lot of things that morning. He thought of his navy days off the New Guinea coast; of ships sinking in fast currents, of wretched men in the water, sunburned, dehydrated, clinging to whatever they could. The sun could kill a person just as fast as the sea, no doubt about it. Well, at least Sue was covered up. He took some consolation in that.

Then his thoughts drifted back to the previous day, to the hammerhead tearing fish from the dive floats, to the tiger shark under the boat. He tried to sweep the images from his mind. He didn't want to confront that possibility. Not yet. Merv stood quietly for a while and watched the breakers charge towards the reef. She might be dead but she could just as well be alive. He wasn't giving up until he knew.

Graham Henderson is Victoria's answer to Merv Sheehan. For the last few years he has served as president of the Australian Underwater Federation and Australia's representative to CMAS, the World Underwater Federation. Needless to say, Graham, or Hendo, as he is more commonly referred to, is a great believer in rules. Without rules there is chaos, and where there is chaos, justice and fair play are little more than words. It is a stance that has won him friends and made him enemies, as he well knows, but he gives no ground. To his supporters the nuggetty Victorian is loyal, forthright and driven. To his critics he is argumentative, opinionated and dogmatic. Either way, those who know him know when the line has been crossed: the arms fold across the chest, the gaze sets on the opponent, the chin tilts upwards slightly. Hendo has dug in for the One Hundred Year War.

Over the past twenty years Hendo has become close friends with Sue and Greg Dockar. But in 1983 his only connection was a few brief hours spent with Greg running the weigh station, and the hideous moment when Sue was pronounced missing.

'I was standing next to Greg in this little boat. I just looked at him and thought, "Oh shit!"'

That evening Hendo, then manager of the Victorian state team, was unceremoniously dumped on Masthead Island with the rest of the horde. He still admits to being somewhat irked by the events of that day and the apparent lack of contingency planning by the Queensland organizers. It was not the way he would have done things. But after a while he accepted that the situation was out of his control so he might as well sit back and enjoy his time on the island.

'It's not something that happens to you every day, now is it?'

Like Vlado and Mark, Hendo woke at dawn. His first task was to make sure all his team were accounted for. Then he gathered them together and instructed them on what they could and couldn't do, namely:

Leave the birds and turtles alone; don't walk on the reef without shoes unless you want a painful, possibly deadly encounter with a stone fish; and under no circumstances is anyone to pick up cone shaped shells, as the poisonous dart inside can kill.

But for Hendo, the most important rule was that they stick together. 'That's what makes you a team', he says. 'That's what makes a team different from everyone else.'

At that point, he recalls, the mood among the castaways was good.

'Most people were from interstate and the "tropical island" thing was not normal to them. There was an air of excitement, excitement like being on a camping trip with kids.'

But by early afternoon food, or more to the point the lack of it, was becoming an issue. Certainly the morning's muster had at least given the castaways some reassurance a meal was on the way; and the game of cricket had served to keep their minds off their stomachs for a while. But the clock was ticking and tensions were growing.

Initially Hendo was too caught up in the island adventure to notice the change in mood. The first inkling of unrest came when he spotted one of the search boats at the edge of the reef. A few of the castaways were unloading what appeared to be boxes of food and drink and wading back across the lagoon. As they came ashore he noticed others emerging from the forest and more approaching from the far end of the beach. Suddenly people were running; grabbing at the boxes, pulling out bread rolls, boiled eggs, pieces of fruit, anything that came to hand and stuffing it into their mouths.

'It was a free-for-all', says one diver. 'A case of "I'm hungry, I want something and I don't give a stuff about anyone else".'

'It was Lord of the Flies stuff', says another. 'I've never seen human beings react like that.'

Hendo stared in disbelief. Then he too was running down the beach. He knew what needed to be done, what needed to be said. By the time he arrived another team manager had already waded into the fray. 'He said: "No! This is not how we're going to do things!" It calmed down after that. A few of us got together and we worked out what food we had and rationed it out fairly.'

The feeding frenzy lasted no more than a few minutes but it was enough to put Hendo on his guard. Almost without thinking he started looking for his team.

'How much does she weigh?'

It was a question Greg had never really considered and certainly not one he was used to discussing with other men. But in the circumstances he had to reply. So he stared at the scruffy hessian sack bulging with lumps of rock and dead coral and tried to equate it with his wife.

'I don't know — nine, nine and a half stone? I don't know.'

The deckhand picked up the sack in an attempt to compare it with the target weight. He frowned and handed it on to the next man who handed it on to the next. They looked at each other then one of them placed another piece of rock in the sack. Then they tied a rope tight around it, wrapped old floats and pieces of tinfoil around its girth and lashed it to a long metal pole.

Reefseeker lumbered around to the northern side of Erskine Island. Greg looked down into the clear blue water and for a moment he imagined Sue hanging on the surface watching the fish as he had seen her do so many times. Then he heard a scraping noise and turned to see the deckhands dragging the sack to the stern. 'It's just a sack', he told himself, as they hurled it into the sea.

It was one o'clock and the tide was high in the lagoon. Turtles basked in the warm shallow water and families of eagle rays swooped beneath the thin veil of blue. But the beauty of the scene barely registered with Greg. When he looked at the island it appeared smaller and more remote than it had the previous day, perhaps because he was aboard *Reefseeker*, perhaps because it was dwarfed by Masthead Island to the west, perhaps because the tiny island made the vastness of the sea so apparent. He didn't know; he didn't care. He just watched the sack bob to the surface, the long pole swinging back and forth like a metronome bar. Within seconds it started to drift.

> *Reefseeker* started to turn around and I assumed we were going to follow the dummy as it travelled. But then I realized we were going back around to the southern side of Erskine Island and next thing the anchor is down and the engines are being switched off. I went straight up to the wheelhouse and asked the skipper why he wasn't following. He said, 'Ah well, there's no point in following it now. We can see it on the radar. We'll give it an hour or two then we'll catch up'.
>
> I could see his point and I knew everything that could be done to find Sue was being done but I hated just sitting there watching the clock, especially when I could see the search boats off in the distance. I just wanted to get out there and feel like I was doing something.
>
> Anyway, an hour or so went by so I went back up to the wheelhouse and the skipper and some other people were up there. I asked if they could turn the radar on. Well, they turned it on and I don't know how much area that thing covered — 3, 4 miles [5 to 7 kilometres] — but we couldn't find the dummy. It had gone off the screen.

The mood on Masthead Island improved considerably once people had eaten, and Hendo started to relax a little. The teams were again together on the beach and, despite the odd rain shower, the noise and smell of the birds, despite everything that had happened, a sense of fun and camaraderie had reignited in the camp.

As for Sue Dockar, she was little more than a backdrop to their own predicament, something beyond their sphere of control, outside their consciousness.

'There was concern, yes, concern that one of our comrades was missing', says Hendo. 'But for 80, 90 per cent of those on the island it was "Sue who?" She was just another diver. Unless you actually knew Sue you wouldn't even picture her.'

After food the most pressing concern on Masthead Island was how to pass the time. They were bored of cricket. Unable to dive, they had explored the island several times over and the novelty of bird watching had well and truly worn off. What they needed was some type of group activity, Hendo could see that.

But when the West Australian team suggested a game of British Bulldog his antennae started to twitch. British Bulldog, also known as Cockie Laura or Red Rover, is a tough schoolyard game. It commences with one person standing in the middle of a delineated 'field' and everyone else at one end. The idea is that the players run from one end of the field to the other while the person in the middle tries to catch as many players as possible as they run past. Those caught join the first person in the middle of the field and the game begins again. The objective is to be the last person caught.

'I said to the Victorians, "Stay out of it, don't anyone play. Just let them go and with any luck they'll injure themselves and won't be able to play in the hockey tournament".'

So Hendo's team sat in a group off to one side and when the game started they cheered and laughed as the runners swerved and sprinted along the beach and those in the middle fought to bring their captives to the ground. But as the game gathered momentum the tackles grew harder, evasion tactics more devious and gradually the laughter died away.

The last five men stood at the end of the beach. No one remembers who made it to the end on that run or how many were caught; but somewhere along the beach three men picked up one of the runners and speared him into the ground.

Hendo didn't realize quite what had happened, just that things had got out of hand again. So he went in to break it up. In fact no one seemed to realize or care that NSW diver Craig Anthony, the man lying motionless on the sand, was unconscious.

'I just blacked out', says Craig.

Then I could hear people saying, 'He's just faking it, he's just faking it', but I couldn't move. I felt incredible pain in my neck. I came round, got up — you know, 'Just a football injury, I'm tough' — and continued to play and catch the last few guys. After that I was in absolute agony.

Six weeks later I found that I had an undisplaced fracture of vertebrae three and four. The bones had cracked virtually all the way round bar a few millimetres. I had a broken neck.

Gunther Pfrengle gets feelings. Not premonitions, or blinding visions, or telepathy, just a sudden, often overwhelming sense that he must be quiet and listen to what his instincts are telling him to do. Such sensations are not uncommon in spearfishing. Plenty of divers talk about feeling a presence then turning to find a shark watching them, or aborting a dive, or not diving at all because something inside said 'no'. Call it a sixth sense; call it a subconscious reaction to slight changes in the environment. All Gunther knew was that over the last twenty-four hours the feelings had come.

The first time was when the search boats anchored off Masthead for the night. It was pitch black and Gunther had lain on the floor of Gerry Hill's boat and tried to sleep. He was sunburnt and sore and the events of the day ran again through his half-conscious brain. Some people thought Sue was dead, he knew that. But the moment his mind fell still he knew she was still out there. He thought about the sharks and it troubled him deeply knowing Sue could neither see them nor defend herself. But it was too dark to search and the men too exhausted to move so he let the thoughts go and fell into an uneasy sleep.

My main memory of that second day was just driving for hours and hours and staring out to sea. My eyes were burning from the salt spray. A lot of the time we saw what we thought was a person, but when we got close it turned out to be a big seabird sitting on the water. That was really annoying as we'd have a search pattern set up, say to cover a 2 kilometre square in 500 metre runs, and every time we investigated one of these sightings it would take us a couple of hundred metres off course.

It was strange being out there and not knowing what everyone else was thinking. I found myself wondering what *Reefseeker* was doing and where they were looking and hoping to God someone was going to come up trumps. One thing that started to worry me was that if Sue didn't come out of this, Merv and a lot of other people would give spearfishing away and I didn't want that to happen. It might sound strange but it made me realize that we had to find Sue for everybody's sake.

Now, sometime that afternoon we received a message asking us to come back to Erskine Island and meet up with the *Reefseeker*. They'd decided to put a dummy in the water with a radar attachment so they could get an idea of the tide and current movements the previous day.

By then conditions had begun to deteriorate. The sea had picked up and there were whitecaps on the waves. That made our job much harder. When the sea is flat you can see a person easily enough, but if there's a bit of wind slop you could be within a hundred metres of them and turn your head for a second and you won't see them.

Anyway, as we came around Masthead Island I had an eerie feeling that there was someone in the water close to the boat.

I was sure I heard something. It was a high-pitched scream or a yell. I kept looking around but I couldn't see anything. I didn't know whether I'd really heard something or if I was imagining it. I thought about saying something to the guys in the boat with me. I looked around but neither of them appeared to have heard anything. I wasn't sure what it was or if it was all in my mind so I let it go.

Sue tried not to think in terms of distance. It didn't mean anything. Neither did time, come to think of it. They were just numbers, measurements, pointless considerations, and if she thought too hard about them the world became a very intimidating place. Instead, she focused on the wide band of green up ahead. That was where she wanted to be and for the first time it felt like conditions were on her side.

I could feel the tide carrying me along and even though I wasn't swimming very fast I felt I was making good progress. I put my head under the water a few times to see if there were any sharks but all I saw was plankton. I dived down a few times too, to see how deep the water was. It wasn't that deep, 40, 50 feet.

As I was swimming these little black birds would swoop overhead and a few times they settled on the water close by. I looked at them and they looked at me and I thought how wonderful it would be to just get up and fly away with them and then I thought about how different everything would look from the sky and what I must look like: this little speck on the water.

It must have been about two o'clock when I really started to feel I had a good chance of reaching Masthead. I could make out the trunks of the trees and the sand on the beach and I reckoned in half an hour I'd be sitting on that beach looking back at the sea, wondering how on earth I'd got into such a mess in the first place.

As I got closer to Masthead it started to rain quite heavily again and the sea became quite choppy. It was hard going because my legs were hurting behind my knees and my back was hurting from holding the buoy and I was taking my fins off all the time because my feet were aching so much. But I didn't want to stop or slow down. I'd just look at that patch of green and think, 'Just keep going, just keep going, it's all going to be over soon'.

I started to hear waves crashing ahead of me. I thought it must be a reef, like the one around Erskine Island and I thought I'd be there in no time at all. There was a heavy swell and it felt like it was coming at me from both sides so I put both my fins on and pushed on. I was sure that if I just kept going I could overcome it.

I don't know when I first noticed it but I started to feel a resistance in the water and it seemed to be growing all the time. It was the same thing I'd felt at Erskine the day before. Then I looked up and realized I wasn't being pushed towards Masthead anymore, the tide had turned and I was getting pushed to the right, away from the island and back out to sea. At that point I just swam as hard as I could. I just kept swimming and swimming and swimming. I didn't care about the pain or the seas; all that mattered was getting to the shore but when I looked up I realized I was still being dragged away from Masthead Island. I put my head down and started swimming again but in the end it was useless because the current was just too strong.

I was really fighting to stay in control and then a boat appeared off to my left, about 500 metres away. It was Don Norman's yellow Shark Cat. I screamed out as loud as I could to be heard over the waves and I was waving my arms frantically. Then I heard an engine roar to my right. I swung around and there was another of the safety boats moving fast around the island. I was screaming and screaming but they didn't hear me. Don's Shark Cat moved across towards the other boat and they went off to the other side of the island.

I guess that was the lowest point for me and as the boats disappeared so did my self-control. I hit the water and I started crying, calling out to God that it wasn't fair, it just wasn't fair. How could he let this happen? For a while I hugged my buoy and cried and just let the waves carry me along. Masthead was just getting smaller and smaller and I knew I had to accept there was nothing I could do about it. I had to prepare myself mentally for another night at sea, but at that moment I wasn't up to it.

It took a while for me to talk myself around. I had to keep telling myself to stay positive and that I was still OK. I wasn't thirsty or hungry, my legs were very sore but I wasn't injured. I was OK and I still had a chance as long as I remained calm.

For the first time that day I let myself take in my surroundings. The seas had calmed down. I was a long way from Masthead again but I could still see it in the distance as the sun started to set. I kept kicking my legs all the time, keeping Masthead in sight as long as possible, but it was hard to tell if I was moving or not any more.

The sunset was beautiful. The clouds on the horizon had broken up into different shapes and distorted faces. The mutton birds seemed to be dive bombing me and I thought about dolphins again. Then it struck me how beautiful everything was and I wished that Greg was with me to see it too. I realized that all my fear and frustration had gone and that I wasn't afraid of death anymore. I thought, 'Well, if it comes out here, then so be it. It's a beautiful place to die'.

POLICE

The next thing he said was, 'There's a 2 metre swell
expected so we want all the boats to go home'.
I said, 'Our guys can handle a 2 metre swell and
we don't intend to go'.

Merv Sheehan

When Sergeant Neville Cooper first arrived in Yeppoon there were
a few things he had to get used to. First, there was the scale of
things. His new patch extended 252 kilometres south to
Bundaberg, 376 kilometres north to the Whitsundays and 313
kilometres out to the Swain Reefs. Then there was the issue of
resources. He'd spent the previous twelve years with Brisbane Water
Police. When an incident occurred off Brisbane he could call on
helicopters, Maritime Services, Fisheries, volunteer rescue, you
name it; as big as Moreton Bay seemed, he could cover just about
every last square metre of it. At the newly established Yeppoon
Water Police Station he could call on his partner, Senior Constable
Noel Perkins, and a 8.5 metre power cat, PW *Cahill*. Two men and
a boat to uphold the law and render assistance on 94,000 square
kilometres of sea.

Then there was the speed of things. It was 8.45 am when Sergeant Cooper received the radio call from Rockhampton District Police: 'Diver missing off Erskine Island since midday the previous day'. He was instructed to proceed to the area and coordinate the search.

At the time he and Senior Constable Perkins were completing a tour of duty off Great Keppel Island some 20 kilometres east of Yeppoon. It would take an hour to return to base, an hour to fuel up and stock the boat with supplies and, even on a good sea, it would be at least four hours before they reached Erskine Island. He knew all too well that when it came to search and rescue time was everything and those first few hours were crucial. After that the search area ballooned out, theories grew like brewer's yeast and as for finding a person alive, you were lucky to find them at all. But orders were orders. Sergeant Cooper confirmed receipt of his instructions and the two men made ready to head south.

Neville Cooper is now retired and lives a quiet life back on the shores of Moreton Bay. But he still remembers the frustration he felt all those years ago.

'Why we weren't sent the information the day before I don't know, because whether it had been daytime or night we would have gone. We were twenty-four hours delayed and that had a huge impact on what we could do.'

Sergeant Cooper didn't know Sue Dockar. She was 'a missing diver', 'an incident' — one of many he had been called to over the years. No offence was meant; it was a necessary mindset, one he could trace back to his very first day on the job. Two ten-year-old boys had gone missing in separate incidents: one was swept away while attempting to cross a flooded river on a horse, the other disappeared while searching for golf balls in a flooded stream. The rookie policeman had been ordered to put on his dive gear and search for them. He never forgot those two lifeless bodies or the grief and despair of their parents. From that day forward he focused his mind on the fundamentals of search and rescue: facts and time. That was the job. So as the two officers travelled out to Erskine

Island they calmly sifted through what information they had and calculated the chances of finding the missing diver alive, dead or not at all. By the time they rendezvoused with *Reefseeker* the appraisal had been done. Senior Constable Perkins brought their boat alongside and Sergeant Cooper jumped across.

Ray Inkpen had spent the better part of the day up in the crows nest. It was not a pleasant place to be, what with the rain and the wind and the roll of the boat, but it was the best vantage point on *Reefseeker*, and for Ray the solitude of the high steel cage provided welcome respite from questions he couldn't answer and gazes he could no longer meet.

The skipper had lent him a pair of binoculars and for the first hour or so he held them to his face, methodically scanning 120 degrees of sea, left to right, left to right, close to the boat, out to the horizon and back again. But the binoculars were large and heavy, and even though he braced himself against the rails of the crows nest, after a while he found he could only hold them to his face for a few minutes at a time. Eventually the burning in his arms and the ache behind his eyes grew too much and he let the binoculars hang around his neck.

She was still alive. Like Ralph and Gunther, he didn't know why he felt so certain — his knowledge of Sue was limited to two brief meetings. But a quiet voice inside declared she was hanging in there, just waiting to be found. He tried to imagine what it would be like for her. What was she thinking? Was she blaming him? God knows he blamed himself, and every time he replayed the events of the previous day the burden grew more onerous.

'I couldn't do enough to keep me happy with my efforts. The only way I could make myself feel good about the whole thing was to be the person who found Sue.'

So he forced himself to search the sea, to stare and stare at everything that might, just might, be a person until it invariably resolved into a white-capped wave, a bird resting on the water or floating rubbish.

By mid-afternoon his time in the crows nest was taking its toll. Ray was tired, sunburned and dehydrated but in spite of Merv's constant nagging he refused to swap places with anyone. The dummy was in the water and, like Greg, Ray needed to see just how far the tide had taken it. Around three o'clock, a blip finally appeared on the edge of the radar screen. *Reefseeker* motored 9 kilometres south-east into an increasingly unsettled swell. When they finally caught up with the dummy Ray turned and looked back to Erskine Island. Even high up in the crows nest the island was little more than a tiny dot in the distance. He knew that Sue, with only her head and shoulders clear of the water, would never have been able to see it.

Sergeant Cooper took charge of the search at 3.50 pm, twenty-five hours and ten minutes after the first alarm was raised. He knew little of the tight-knit world he had entered, but he was all too familiar with the scene: the solemn mood, the drawn faces, the desperate look in the eyes of people hoping against hope.

As search coordinator his first task was to avail himself of the circumstances of the disappearance, the resources available and the search area covered to date. A young man came forward and introduced himself as Ray Inkpen, convenor of the competition. Merv Sheehan stood close behind. They ushered Sergeant Cooper into *Reefseeker*'s main cabin. Within minutes the searchers had gathered around and their story came pouring out.

'To the credit of the people who were there they were doing as good as they could do', he says now. He looks down at a chart of the Capricorn Group and points to the channels flanking Erskine Island.

'Through there it can reach speeds of 3 knots without any trouble at all. That means by the time they really realized what was going on she would have been miles away.'

Sergeant Cooper detailed Senior Constable Perkins and one of *Reefseeker*'s crew to search the waters south-east, south and south-west in the police boat. The five power boats were directed to search the waters to the east, north-east and north-west. As for *Reefseeker*, the dummy was still travelling south-east at around 2.5 knots and for the time being they would continue to monitor its course.

When Greg Dockar heard the police were on their way his immediate question was, 'How soon?' There was a sense of urgency in his voice that even he could hear; a desperate belief that their arrival would inject new momentum into the search and Sue would be found. He clung to that notion right up until the moment Sergeant Cooper stepped on board.

> That's when he started shooting his mouth off. He said, 'She's lost now and she's bloody drowned. Now we've got to do a search to find a body!'
>
> I couldn't say anything. I just stood there trying to take in what he had said. How could he just write her off like that? He didn't know Sue. He didn't know us!

For Greg Dockar the next few hours passed in a blur, as if he were flicking through the story of someone else's hell; people shouting, the dummy being dragged from the water, the constant drone of *Reefseeker*'s engines.

He was oblivious to his own state. All he knew was they weren't looking for a person any more; they were looking for a body, the body of his wife.

Neville Cooper remembers it very differently.

> I wouldn't have said it in those terms. I wouldn't use terminology like that. I'd have said it's most likely that we're looking for a body and I think everybody agreed with me at that time. It was just stating the obvious.

They were miles offshore. The diver had been officially missing for twenty-six hours, and not seen for thirty-three. The chances of finding her alive were slim: simple as that.

Her husband, he was remaining positive. He was quite adamant that she wouldn't give up and that sort of kept us in the area and we certainly weren't calling anything off and closing it down.

Sergeant Cooper asked for volunteers qualified to use scuba equipment, to search the waters around Erskine Island. No one mentioned bodies, at least not in front of Greg. Officially they were looking for dive gear, Sue's weight belt in particular. That would tell them her position when she first got into trouble.

There are certain privileges that go with rank and for Hendo one of those was being able to cadge a lift over to *Reefseeker* when a search boat stopped in at Masthead Island.

He wasn't quite sure what to expect when he climbed aboard, although getting a cup of coffee and catching up with Merv were high on his agenda. The last thing he anticipated was for Merv to 'volunteer' him for the search.

I remember it was late in the afternoon and the tide was running. We were all standing there kitted up on the duckboard about to swim across to the police launch. It must have only been 6, maybe 8 metres away; I jumped in close to the bow of the police launch and I only just made the stern — and I had fins and all!

Officially, those on *Reefseeker* and the safety boat crews were still searching the seas for an orange buoy and a bobbing head. Unofficially, the notion that Sue had been taken by the current had been usurped by a growing belief that she had been taken by a shark. But it was only as the police launch neared Erskine Island that Hendo and the other volunteers aboard began to contemplate the grim reality of their task.

> We thought if she'd been caught in the current we might find a weight belt but if she'd been taken by a shark we might find a flipper with a foot still in it or part of her body with the weight belt around and I can't say any of us wanted to be the one to find that.

The police launch motored over to the northern side of the island, to the last place Sue had been seen. As the volunteers put on their dive tanks Senior Constable Perkins issued their instructions. They were to conduct a sweep around the island. Because of the currents they were to stay in a line, holding hands and searching the area within their arm span. That line was not to be broken unless a positive sighting was made. He would follow a distance behind in the boat.

Hendo holds conflicting memories of that dive. He recalls the beauty of the coral, yet he also remembers how the sheer power of the outgoing tide meant that on occasions he and others had to break the line and drag themselves along the bottom. At the back of his mind were the tales of sharks ripping fish from people's rigs, and as he swam along the bottom he found himself wondering what it would be like to be torn apart by such a creature. Would death be prolonged and agonizing or would the sheer ferocity of such an attack kill instantly? Either way, he knew if he came across Sue's body, or part of it, he would never be able to dive the reef again.

'It was a surreal feeling you know; diving in this beautiful water over this fantastic coral and it's all great and I'm thinking, "If I find an arm or a leg I'm going to be so annoyed!"'

The divers combed the reefs and bomboras for more than an hour but found no sign of Sue; and to the great relief of all concerned, no evidence of shark attack. As the sun began to set they went ashore just in case. They checked the beaches and the scrub, and the shallow pool of the lagoon.

'We didn't find anything', says Hendo. 'No dive gear, no footprints, nothing.'

Reefseeker arrived off Masthead Island a little after 8.30 pm. The police boat *Cahill* and the five safety boats arrived soon after. Ralph Whalley, Tim Paulsen and John Powell climbed aboard *Reefseeker* and joined the search team in the main cabin. Those present say Ralph 'wasn't happy'. To anyone who knows the man those words speak volumes. Truth be known, Ralph had been stewing ever since the police had taken over the search. He had pretty much taken an instant dislike to 'that sergeant' and he didn't approve of his manner or his methods, not one bit.

'That tide had been running out for the better part of the afternoon', says Ralph. 'Unless Sue was part Atlantic salmon and she could swim against a 3 knot current that meant she'd be heading out with it — out to the south-east!'

But Ralph felt as though his insights were being blankly ignored: he and the other safety boats were promptly sent — ordered, no less — to go north, and that annoyed him no end.

The evening meeting did little to improve his mood. He didn't care for all the talk about 'bottom searches' and 'body recoveries'. Sue was alive and he was going to find her and that was that. But there were other things to consider. First and foremost, the weather was turning bad and there were people on Masthead Island who had little food and no shelter. For the safety of all concerned Sergeant Cooper wanted them picked up and returned to Gladstone later that night.

Sitting across the table from Ralph was an ashen-faced Merv Sheehan. His statement to police indicates that by late that evening he too had grudgingly admitted Sue 'may have been attacked by a large shark'. But it is not in Merv's nature to accept defeat, no matter how inevitable it might seem.

> I said we weren't going to go away until we found some evidence. We had done a search all around the island and we didn't find any gear at all. That meant she could still have her gear with her and that meant she could still be alive.

Eventually, what appeared to be a compromise was reached. The people on Masthead Island would be picked up on the high tide due around midnight. *Reefseeker* would then return to Gladstone. The police boat and the five safety boats would remain behind and resume the search at first light.

The news reached the Masthead Island castaways long before *Reefseeker* weighed anchor off the reef. One of the safety boats dropped in and told them Sue had not been found, so they were all heading back to Gladstone. It wasn't long before the news was translated: Sue was dead.

Vlado cannot recall feeling grief. 'I don't think it really hit us, not on the island.'

The sun was going down over Masthead Island and the massive reef flat was once again little more than a shallow pool, but the mood of the sea was shifting. What in the morning had been their playground was now the perimeter of their fortress; a wild, windswept no-man's land between them and the constant onslaught of angry, white-capped waves.

No one smiled and few spoke as they sat on the beach and watched the sun go down. For a few moments the sea and sky turned gold and blood red and the bellies of the storm clouds burned orange. Then the sun dropped beneath the horizon and the world turned pitch black. The mutton birds howled and the campfire glowed.

'The main thing I remember is dinner', says Vlado.

Peter Inskip — he was cooking the soup or whatever we had. He'd mixed up everything we'd caught that day in one big pot — whole garfish, the rays and squid and all sorts of peppery stuff. By the time we were ready to eat it was dark. Then we realized we had no plates so we were all running around in the dark looking for clam shells to eat off. We all had to line up. He said, 'You can come up and grab a shellfull but you're not allowed to shine a torch inside the pot'. It tasted good, really good.

Unlike the chaotic scenes earlier in the day, their last meal on the island was an orderly, communal affair. As one person finished their ration, they went down to the sea, rinsed out the shell and handed it on to the next person. When the soup was gone people lingered around the campfire, whiling away their last few hours talking, playing cards, staring into the flames. For a while the juniors played poker off in a little group of their own. It was something to do and Mark in particular needed to keep his mind occupied. Whether it was loyalty or instinct, he was not ready to accept that Sue was dead. But every so often the grim campfire conversations of shark attack and drowning would intrude into the game. Eventually the intrusion grew too much. The boys showed their hands and disappeared into the darkness.

The calendar of the Capricorn Group is marked just as much by the cycle of life as it is by the trade winds and cyclones that march across its skies — the migration of humpback whales; the summer influx of noddy terns and shearwaters; but perhaps more than anything by the turtle season. Green and loggerhead turtles start appearing around the coral cays in late September, some having travelled thousands of kilometres from Arnhem Land, New Guinea, New Caledonia and Fiji. The females are sexually active for a little over a week, the males for around a month. Between November and

March the females come ashore in the cool of the evening to lay their eggs. It is one of the great rituals of nature and one the boys were determined to see before they left the island.

They found themselves a spot high up the beach out of the wind and for a while they watched and waited. They couldn't see the waves but they could hear them in the distance — a boom followed by the sound of thousands of tonnes of water thundering over coral. When they shone their torches out over the reef flat they discovered the wind had strafed even those waters with white crests of sea foam and they wondered if it could be too rough for the turtles to venture over the reef. Then their lights touched on a black mound moving steadily towards the beach. The boys turned off their torches. A few moments later a turtle lumbered out of the surf and lay on the beach. Then she raised her head and started to haul her massive frame up past the high water mark and into the scrub.

'The older blokes said we were to stay out of the way until they started digging their hole, otherwise they'd get spooked and take off', says Mark.

> Anyway we sat there and waited a few minutes and then we crept down and sat next to her. It was awesome. I don't think any of us had seen a turtle before that comp, maybe on TV or in a zoo or something, but not up close, and there we were sitting there, right next to her, and it was like she didn't even notice us.

For the next few hours thoughts of death were pushed aside as the turtle used her giant flippers to scoop out and compress the sand beneath her. Quite how she knew what to do was a mystery. Scientists say female sea turtles are at least fifty years old before they mate and lay their first clutch of eggs. Fifty years on the open sea with no pod, school or colony to protect them or learn from. Yet somehow the knowledge is passed on. The boys didn't know how old the turtle was or where she had travelled from; just that she kept digging until the hole was roughly as wide and as deep as her massive shell. Then she climbed up onto the side of the hollow and a few moments later soft-shelled eggs began to fall from her body.

> It's pretty weird. Everyone was down because it looked like Sue was dead and there we were watching turtles nesting, you know, the beginning of life. And it wasn't just that one turtle. We got to witness about ten coming up on the beach that night.

'We lay there for hours just watching them digging their holes and laying their eggs', says Mark.

For Vlado and Scottie it was all part of the adventure, yet another story to tell the folks back home. But for Mark the truly defining moment of those two days came a little after midnight when he looked up from the turtle hollow and saw the lights of the safety boats on the edge of the reef.

> We were looking out at this howling sou'easter and regardless of whether you thought Sue had got taken by a shark, all I could think was how could anyone — anyone — survive such conditions: whitecap after whitecap just slapping you in the back of the head, not just for a couple of hours but day in, day out. I couldn't comprehend how anyone could be out in that sea and survive.

LAST HOPE

The one thing that doesn't abide by majority rule is a person's conscience.

Harper Lee, To Kill a Mockingbird

Reefseeker started taking on passengers around midnight. For the four NSW juniors it marked the end of their island adventure. But for Greg Dockar the return of the castaways meant something quite different.

> You know you're being watched. But you know you just can't hide. You can't. They'd be looking at you and seeing what the reaction is of someone who's just lost their wife. You know what I mean. It was sort of like being on display. In the end I couldn't hack it. I said to the captain, 'Where can I hide?'

Greg Dockar was placed in the crews quarters behind the wheelhouse. He could shut the door on the world but he could not shut off his despair. He knew that in the minds of those below Sue was already dead, but in his mind she was still very much alive.

'It was like someone telling you your arm's been cut off but you can still feel the fingers moving', he said.

When the anchor chain came up and *Reefseeker* started its journey back to Gladstone, Greg felt he had committed the greatest act of desertion in his life. The fact that he had no say in it was irrelevant. He was leaving his wife to die.

Ray Inkpen was faring little better. As the castaways came back onboard he stood at the stern and ticked off their names to ensure no one was left behind. He hoped for just one kind word, one signal of support, but in the faces of long-time friends all he saw was resentment, anger and disappointment. And he knew it would only get worse.

A woman was missing, presumed dead and everybody was looking at me. I'd been told there'd be a coroner's inquest and they'd wipe the floor with me. As it was, I blamed myself for just about everything.

I really don't know what I felt but I felt shithouse. If I could have jumped over the side of the boat and disappeared with Sue I would have been real happy with that.

Ralph had a bad feeling and it wasn't about Sue. He sensed the police were going to call off the search.

In theory, even if he was right, there was no action he could take. But Ralph never did have much time for theories and in his view there was something he could do. In fact, he'd already done it. Earlier that evening he'd snuck over to Heron Island and refuelled his boat and taken on a little more besides, and when the other search boats headed east to Heron for the night he turned west and anchored up behind Masthead. If it came to it, they could keep searching for another day and the cops would be none the wiser.

There were just the three of them in the boat now. Paul Riorden had shifted over to John Powell's boat to help sort out some engine trouble. Ralph, Tim and Andy were huddled in the half cabin out of the wind. There was no food left so they smoked cigarettes and downed the remains of a bottle of rum. For all three, but for Ralph in particular, the matter had gone beyond personal. He kept telling everyone: forget the sharks, they'll leave her alone, as for the sea state, he'd dived in worse and had no doubt Sue had too.

'It was the middle of bloody summer. It was like bathwater out there and she had a wetsuit on so she could bob around for days', he says.

Some say he was just plain stubborn. Maybe, but on this occasion he was also right. The water temperature at the time was 27 degrees Celsius. According to the Australian Maritime Safety Authority, 'It is generally assumed that at sea temperatures in excess of 21 degrees, survival time is indefinite providing there is no danger from sharks and the person can stay afloat.'

The plan was mapped out: up before dawn again, then out round Masthead and over to Erskine. It was going to be a horrible sea, but the tide would be coming back in and she'd be coming in with it. If Ralph was right, and he knew he was, they'd have searched half the Capricorn Group and found Sue before the coppers were out of bed.

'The old memory's starting to clear a bit now', says Neville Cooper.

'We'd anchored off Masthead that night and the wind came up about one or two o'clock in the morning. We were on the wrong side of the island and we had to up-anchor and get in the lee.'

Neither he nor Perkins had any inkling of Ralph's plans. At that point their main concern was that it had been a long hard day and the coming one would be no different. All they wanted was a safe anchorage and a good night's sleep. But Sergeant Cooper was certainly aware a few people weren't happy. Did it bother him? Not at all: in his experience some people supported the police, some people hated them. That was just the way it was, particularly up in that neck of the woods.

At that stage the new Water Police Station at Yeppoon had only been open a matter of months. In that time they'd found out just how hard small towns can be on outsiders, particularly those they view as city boys. And the hardest people to get on side were the trawler fishermen, the professional fishermen: 'They're a tough breed.'

The two officers knew it would pass; that eventually they would come through all their tests. But in those early days, the only friends they had — the only people they could truly call upon — were each other. That night was fairly typical. They made sure the anchor was holding, crawled into their bunks and in that twilight time between wake and sleep they talked over the events of the day.

One thing played on Neville Cooper's mind: the missing woman's husband, Greg Dockar, and his constant assertion that his wife was a very strong swimmer. For Sergeant Cooper that ability related to distance swimming, and distance swimming equated to mental strength; there in the darkness, he considered the possibility that it could mean sufficient strength to survive.

> I said to my partner, 'She could still be alive'. He said, 'She's in a wetsuit, she's got buoyancy'. I said, 'She could bob up somewhere, barring any marine accident, sharks or something like that coming along'.

Then they listened to the wind howling around the boat and the distant sound of waves crashing onto coral, and they, like Mark Colys, found themselves wondering how anyone at all could survive in such conditions. A few moments later the men were asleep.

Sue Dockar resigned herself to a second night in the water long before the sun went down. She knew that without the current behind her she would never make it back to Masthead Island. After a while she stopped swimming and just let the waves carry her along.

I remember feeling very relaxed and being content to just take in the final moments of the day. I don't know if it was my state of mind or that it was the first time it had really hit me how magnificent the sea was and how peaceful it was. I was out of the heavy wave sets and back in a long, constant swell. The main thing I remember is watching the birds gliding over the waves, and tracing animals and people's faces in the clouds.

I took one last look around for boats and planes as the sun went down. I saw what looked like a fishing boat a long way off. It didn't seem to be moving, so I called out to it as loud as I could but there was no reply. I kept calling. Then the sun went down and Masthead and the boat disappeared. I could hear the waves all around but I couldn't see them any more. I could feel the sea but didn't know where it was taking me. For a while I just hung in the water lying across my buoy. I took a few deep breaths and kept reassuring myself I was OK and that at least this time I knew what to expect. The most important thing was to accept the night and not fight it or be afraid.

A bit later on I noticed lights appearing all around me. I thought they must be fishing boats, all of them a long way off, but I began to swim to what I thought was the closest, brightest light. By that stage there was no skin left on my heels and it felt as if someone was trying to bury a hot poker in the back of my neck. I knew I couldn't carry on for much longer but I kept going.

About an hour or so later I felt the current start to move so I swam with it. It was hard to tell where I was being taken, but I remembered Ralph saying how the currents run back and forth on the same course and I was hoping this one would take me back to Masthead. I swam for a while, trying not to look down into the black water or think about the pain I was in.

Then I heard what I thought sounded like a dog howling and I stopped swimming and looked around. It was a really a strange noise, sort of out of place on the reef and I was thinking, 'What would a dog be doing out here?' I thought it might be on someone's boat or it might be someone in a boat messing around so I called out in the direction of the noise but there was no answer and after a while the noise stopped.

I don't know what happened next, I think I must have had a dream or hallucination. All I can tell you is that it felt real and I'll never forget it. I was floating above the waves, looking down at someone in the water. The person was lifeless, just hanging onto the buoy, face down in the black sea. After a few moments I realized it was me. I wasn't dead; I was staring at something. I looked past me and into the water. I could see a village down on the sea floor. There were lights on in the houses and people were walking on the streets, and old-fashioned cars drove through the village — you know, the type the gangsters used to drive in the 1930s. I felt very warm and relaxed and I was quite happy to just hang there and watch. Then I heard a man's voice — it sounded very calm and reassuring. He told me it was alright, I should let go of the buoy and everything would be alright.

He said it a few times. I couldn't see his face, I just heard the voice. It sounded real and I wanted to believe in him but I knew deep down it had to be a dream. I kept saying, 'No, I don't believe you'. He kept talking in the same reassuring tone. He said it was OK, the sea would part and we could go down to the village. I said, 'Prove it to me'. The voice kept telling me to let go of the buoy and I kept saying 'No'. I remember physically shaking my head and saying, 'No, no, that's not right'. Then I woke up. It was dark and I was still in the water.

As the night wore on I felt the mood of the sea begin to change. At first it wasn't too bad, the swell was getting bigger, but I wasn't being thrown about too much. By early morning it was rough. I mean, we're not talking hurricane conditions or anything but you really wouldn't choose to be out in a sea like that. Waves were coming at me from everywhere. I was really getting knocked around and it wasn't long before I lost all sense of direction. I could feel myself being dragged along very fast, but I had no idea where I was heading. All of my concentration was focused on keeping hold of my buoy and bracing myself for the next wave, and the next, and the next. I had no time to think positive, or reassure myself that I was OK. I wasn't. All I could do was hang on to my buoy and hope the sea would calm down, but if anything it was getting worse. One wave hit me so hard it nearly ripped my face mask off. I grabbed the strap of the mask and pulled it tight until it hurt. I just couldn't afford to loose the mask because without it I was blind, and out there if I was blind I was as good as dead.

It got a bit better when the sun came up. At least then I could see what I was up against and ride the waves instead of being hit by them. Occasionally when a wave picked me up I'd catch glimpses of the horizon. At that point there was no land in sight, just this very intimidating sea. Everywhere I looked waves were roaring along and tumbling into one another. I looked around for boats and planes but I couldn't see any and to me that seemed strange. I'd seen search planes very early the previous day and I wondered if they'd been delayed for some reason — then I realized that the search had probably been called off.

I remember thinking about Greg and Merv and Ralph and I couldn't believe they'd given up on me. It's not something we do. Then I looked at the sea again and I thought, 'Who in their right mind would be searching in this weather and even if they were still searching, how could they spot me in this sea?' Then a big wave came crashing down — it really knocked the wind out of me. I remember scrambling to the surface and then another wave came through but I managed to catch that one before it broke. At that point I started to question how much more I could take. I knew I was exhausted and I needed to sleep and it crossed my mind how easy it would be to let go of the buoy. It was only brief but it woke me up. I knew I just couldn't do that. I'd never just give up and die.

For a while I just held onto my buoy and did my best to anticipate the sea and ride it out. I felt very numb. I had no concept of distance or time, just waves, and I tried to focus on the happy times Greg and I had had together. The next thing I remember is a big wave coming through and sweeping me upwards. As it peaked I looked out across the horizon. I caught a brief glimpse of a patch of gold before I fell into the wave trough. Then another wave came through and I struggled to catch it. As the wave peaked I saw the patch of gold again. I thought, 'My God, it's sand!' I told myself to calm down, but instinctively I started to swim.

I was telling myself not to get my hopes up, because I'd come so close the day before and didn't make it and the same thing might happen again. But all I could think was it might be the last chance I had. The sea was behind me and I had to make the most of it.

I don't know how long I swam for, an hour, maybe two, but after a while I began to hear waves crashing and I realized there must be a reef ahead. At first it didn't register, or I wouldn't let it, but the noise steadily grew louder and then it dawned on me that I had to go over the reef to get to land. I thought, 'I've survived all this just to get ripped apart on a reef', and I stopped swimming, hoping that would slow me down and give me some control. But the waves were dragging me along. I was going on to the reef whether I liked it or not so I thought, 'OK, let's go with it'. I started to swim again, but this time much harder. The noise of the waves was quite intimidating and the movement was quite violent.

I felt a surge of water behind me and the wave lifted me up high and dropped into white water. I knew the next wave would put me on the reef so I pulled my buoy underneath me and braced myself for the impact. I was sure that I'd break something or get dragged over the coral. I felt the wave come through, it hurled me upwards, then down towards the reef. I remember the coral rushing towards my face. Then, when I was literally inches off the coral the wave broke. I clung to my buoy and kicked as hard as I could. Another wave came through which picked me up and threw me over the reef. I could still hear the waves, but suddenly the water was still and clear.

I'd made it.

GOING NOWHERE

Nobody wanted to let it go. We were all experienced seamen and Sue was an experienced diver and we knew there was a good chance that she would still be alive.

Gunther Pfrengle

The channel between Polmaise Reef and Masthead Island is known as 'the race track' in reference to the currents that scream through it at anything up to 5 knots. This is useful information, because if a man knew the area well enough, if he understood how the currents moved and how a strong sou'easterly wind swept around Masthead Island, he might (if he did not want to disturb the sleeping occupants of a nearby police launch) be able to up anchor and let the elements carry his Shark Cat some distance before he had to switch his engines on. No one is saying that was what happened, because flouting a direct police order 'to stay at anchor and await instructions' could be deemed an offence. But it might explain how, for a few hours at least, Ralph Whalley, Tim Paulsen and Andy Ruddock managed to evade the long arm of the law.

What is known is that the three men were under way shortly after sun-up, and that as they came around the northern tip of

Masthead Island they met the weather head on — 2 to 3 metre waves, pushed along by 25 knot winds gusting at around 30 knots. In the realm of commercial, even recreational fishing such conditions are considered workable, but this was day three of a search for a missing diver and sea conditions, according to the subsequent police report, were 'rough with visibility next to nil'.

When Ralph's boat reached Erskine Island the first task was to check in case Sue had come ashore. It was too rough to bring the boat in close so he kept the Shark Cat in the lee of the island while Andy and Tim put on their masks and fins and swam in. Twenty minutes later they climbed back on board, reporting no signs of life. Ralph motored slowly around the island — once, twice. A search plane circled high overhead. The wind howled and wild waves thundered over the south-east rim of Erskine lagoon. The radio crackled and the voice of Sergeant Cooper barked into the boat. They ignored it and motored around the island for a third time.

'We knew she was on her way in and all we had to do was keep searching in that area', says Ralph.

At around 6.30 am Tim announced they had company. Ralph looked back and saw the police launch heading their way and he turned the radio up. All Ralph will say is the police 'weren't very happy with them' and they were instructed to proceed to Heron Island. Andy says Ralph was furious — they all were. 'None of us wanted to leave Erskine but the decision wasn't ours to make.'

They took one last look around Erskine Island. Then Ralph turned the boat around and they punched into the swell.

Sue Dockar tumbled over the south-east rim of Erskine lagoon around 7.30 am. She had no idea where she was, but that could wait. The only thing that mattered was she was alive.

As soon as I came over the reef I knew I was going to be OK. It was like suddenly my whole body, my mind, everything, just relaxed all at once. I knew I was safe and I could see the beach not too far away so for a while I just let myself float along. There were lots of little fish in among the coral and then a little further in a turtle swam past and I saw a few larger fish. I was very, very tired and I realized my lips were cracked and swollen and that the saltwater really hurt. But I also knew there would be no food on the island so I loaded my gun and tried to shoot a fish. I missed and then they all took off. At that point I decided I'd had enough and headed into shore.

The beach was quite steep and I was so weak I had to crawl up on my hands and knees. Until then I just hadn't realized how weak I was. When I got clear of the water I tried to stand up again but I couldn't do it. In the end I just sat down on the sand and waited for my strength to come back.

I don't know how long I was there for. I just sat there looking at the sea and the waves crashing over the reef and wondering how I came through it in one piece, and feeling very grateful that I had. The main thing was I knew I had a much better chance of survival on land, and that I'd be much easier to spot.

I started taking off my wetsuit. I had to do it very slowly because I couldn't stand up. The thing that stays in my mind is how wrinkled my skin was. I pulled my dive gloves off and my hands were all wrinkled and white. Then when I took off my skivvy and my wetsuit longjohn I realized my whole body was like that. I thought about how Merv nagged me to cover up before the comp. Well, he'd been right to do that because I started to think how bad my skin would have been if he hadn't. As it was, the only place I had sunburn was around my wrist in the gap between my skivvy sleeve and my glove.

I also became aware that everything seemed to hurt. The area behind my knees had been hurting for the last couple of days but it was only once I'd got the wetsuit off that I realized sores had formed where it had chafed on my legs. They were deep and looked quite nasty but there wasn't much I could do apart from try and keep the sand out of them.

Eventually I managed to get up and I walked rather unsteadily up the beach. I hung my wetsuit and skivvy on a tree to dry and laid my other gear on some scrub. I put my buoy high up on the sand so it could be seen and made sure the dive flag was flying on it. I didn't have my glasses of course so I kept my dive mask with me and held it up to my face so I could see. I walked along and found some branches and pieces of driftwood. I used them to write 'HELP' in big letters on the sand. I really was unsteady on my feet so I kept one of the branches and used it for support as I continued on around the island.

I got a little further down the beach and that's when I saw another island off in the distance. At the time I didn't know where I was but as soon as I saw the other island I knew it was Masthead. Then I realized I must be on Erskine Island, the very island I started from. A lot of things went through my mind when I realized where I was, not the least of which was Ralph had been so right about the currents and I'd been right to believe him. At the time I thought how good it would be to tell him that personally.

I could see footprints in the sand and I found a broken divers flag and a rubber from someone's speargun. I picked them up thinking I could return them to their owners when I was found. A little further down the beach I found a drink container with the lid on, with about an inch of water left in it, and I picked that up too.

I kept walking around until I was back where I started from. All that time in the water I had to stay alert. Now I was on land I just wanted to lie down and I let the exhaustion take over for a while. I found a hollow under a large bush and crawled in, putting the drink bottle in the shade next to me making sure it would not fall over or get hot. I was quite thirsty but I knew that I had to make the water last as long as possible so I just used it to wet my lips.

I was tired but I was so stiff and sore it was hard to sleep — I had to keep moving all the time because it felt like if I didn't I'd set in the one spot. Then just when I'd get comfortable the sun would come through the branches and I'd have to move again to stay in the shade. I'm making it sound like a big deal and it wasn't really. I'd seen the helicopters flying around for the last couple of days so I was sure somebody would fly over and see me even if it was not that day. The main thing I needed was to rest and stay out of the sun so that's what I tried to do. I was very happy to be alive. When I thought about my time in the water it all seemed a long way away.

As Ralph motored towards Heron Island *Reefseeker* arrived back at Gladstone. It had been a rough, uncomfortable trip and the mood onboard was as heavy and sullen as the rain clouds that hung over the harbour. Gladstone had seen its share of wild weather over recent days. Storms had dumped 196.7 millimetres of rain over the town in the previous twenty-four hours, 209 millimetres in the last seventy-two, filling the new 44,000 megalitre dam to overflowing.

It was 7.30 am. Greg Dockar remained in the crews quarters until *Reefseeker* came alongside the wharf. Only then did he walk out to the wheelhouse and look down at the people gathered there. He recognized a few familiar faces — mainly the family and friends of spearos. But there were also strangers among them: bystanders, journalists, police.

'They hung around like bloody vultures. I mean, what did they expect to see? I told Merv, "I want everyone to go ashore. I'm not going out there until everyone's gone".'

He waited on the upper deck as people filed off the boat, as the crowd slowly dispersed, until the last journalist got into his car and drove away. Still he lingered. Then a woman called his name.

Gunther's wife, Nada, she'd come on board. I didn't know Nada very well before that — I think we'd met briefly before I went out on the boat — but she came straight up to me and gave me a big hug.

They sat for a while and Greg poured out his heart. All Nada could do was listen. Eventually she told him it was time to leave. She picked up the small holdall Sue had packed three days earlier. She found Sue's dive bucket and spare gear still tucked under a seat on the stern deck. Between them, Nada and Greg carried the last relics of Sue Dockar off the boat.

At 9 am on 4 January 1983 Sergeant Cooper called all the search crews together at Heron Island. He announced that due to the weather conditions he was calling off the sea search for the time being. The five-boat search team was to return to Gladstone as soon as weather permitted. Resort manager Brian Edmonds and the manager of Lloyd Helicopters, David Hogan, had agreed to continue searching from the air during scheduled flights to and from Heron Island. The police boat would be on hand in case they sighted anything in the water or the weather improved enough for the sea search to resume.

'Some people were angry', says Neville Cooper.

They thought the search should have kept going. Mind you, a lot of those people just don't know the conditions in the area. You don't risk other people's lives. How many lives do you risk to save one? That is what you have got to keep adding up.

Ralph Whalley, Tim Paulsen and John Powell were adamant they knew the waters and could handle the conditions. But Sergeant Cooper would not give ground.

It is always a tough decision and it's always got to be calculated and based on fact. And the fact was we couldn't search that area without risking further life. Also, it was the third day and the chances of Sue being alive were slim. So, do you risk lives to look for a body?

He instructed Brian Edmonds to provide the crews with enough fuel to return to Gladstone — no more, no less. Precisely what Ralph said to Sergeant Cooper remains between the two of them. Andy described the exchange as a 'long and loud list of expletives'.

'Ralph was absolutely gutted, we all were', he said.

Ray Inkpen's welcoming committee in Gladstone consisted of two young police officers. They informed Ray he would be facing a coroner's inquest and told him to report to the police station later that day.

Next came the journalists with their questions and their cameras. Thankfully, Merv took centre stage on that occasion because some of those questions — well, most of them in fact — Ray hadn't come to terms with himself yet. Merv wasn't doing much better but at least he got rid of the reporters, leaving one particular photographer in no doubt where his lens would end up if he didn't move on.

Finally, there was Ray's girlfriend, Helen. For the past three days she had followed the progress of the search via news reports and snippets of information gleaned from the Port Curtis Volunteer Air Sea Rescue. But nothing quite prepared her for the look on Ray's face. All she could do was be there for him but Ray could not let his feelings out: 'I still had a job to do'.

Helen drove him back to Tannum Sands and despite her pleas for him to take at least a short break, he showered, shaved and walked over to the office. Competition flyers, information sheets, championship T-shirts still sat in the same neat piles he'd arranged before he left. The only thing different was the newspapers on the desk. He picked up that morning's edition. The lead story reported on the flooding in the area caused by the heavy rain and high tides. At the bottom of the page was the headline, 'Diving Mishap'. The small box of text described how an air and sea search was continuing for a woman skindiver, 'Sue Docker', missing since Sunday. At first Ray felt like phoning the newspaper up and telling them 'the real story' — that in his opinion the police had given up too soon. But then he looked closer and decided there was no point. 'They couldn't even spell her name right.'

For a while Ray tried to shut the last few days out of his mind and attend to other matters. But it wasn't long before a small delegation walked in and brought him back to reality.

> You'd think by now that everyone would have cooled off to the idea of a second day of competition. But they were worrying about what was going to happen to the second day and were we going to hold it. I couldn't believe it. What's more, I couldn't stomach it. I told them I didn't want anything at all to do with it and I was quite relieved when Merv and a few others came in and said there was no way we were going to have another spearing comp.

The delegation left the office soon after. Ray Inkpen has not spoken to any of them since.

By mid-morning it was getting hot on Erskine Island and although she had sworn she would not get back in the water for some time, the heat eventually coaxed Sue from her hollow and down to the lagoon. She was too stiff to swim and even the smallest amount of saltwater hurt her swollen and blistered lips. But the lagoon was cool and calm and for the time being she was content just to sit in the water and watch the waves crash onto the reef.

The noise of the waves was always there, it didn't matter where I was on the island. I'd got up a few times thinking a boat or a plane was in the area, but I'd realized it was just the sea. I'd think, boy I'm really glad I'm not out in that anymore. But at that stage the main thing on my mind was water — I was getting quite hungry too — but water was definitely my main concern.

I got up from the lagoon and decided to go for another walk around the island. I'd never done any survival courses or anything like that. I'd seen a couple of things on TV about how people in the desert collect rainwater using sheets of plastic and things but I didn't have any of that stuff. All I had was my mask and my little Orchy bottle which I carried with me everywhere. I found lots of bits of rubbish on the island, lots of cans and bottles. I must have looked in every single one of them, hoping I'd find something I could drink, but all I found in them was sand and a few drops of foul-smelling liquid.

I found more bits of driftwood and used them to write HELP a few more times on the sand. Then I walked around again trying to find something to drink. I'd seen tracks as I was walking around the island and I thought, well if it comes to it I'll try and dig up some eggs. I didn't really want do that if I didn't have to — even back then turtles were endangered. Also I didn't know if I had the strength to do it, so digging up turtle eggs really would be a last resort. I remember at one point looking at some of the plants on the island and wondering if they were edible or if I could get juice from some of the more thick-leafed plants. I did break a few leaves off but they didn't smell very nice and in the end I decided it was best not to try them as I didn't want to poison myself at that stage. I went a bit further into the scrub and I came across this red and white pole sticking up in the middle of the island and I thought maybe the guys might have left some food or water for me but there was nothing. In the end there was nothing for it: I found the turtle hollow and started digging in the sand with my hands.

It was hard work and it wasn't long before I started getting hot and tired so I decided to leave it for a while and I went into the water again to cool down.

By then I was very thirsty and conscious that I was badly dehydrated and I knew I had to find fresh water or some type of fluid soon. It sounds weird I know but at the same time I was sitting in the lagoon looking around at the sea and the island thinking that in the right circumstances it would be a lovely place to stay for a while, you know, camp out. It had nice beaches, beautiful coral, good fishing. Of course next time I'd have to remember to bring the food hamper with me.

Greg Dockar was back at Tannum Sands. Nada had told him to take a shower and change but when he went back to 'their' room and started looking for his clothes he became aware of Sue's shoes under the bed, her favourite beach towel over the chair, the dress she had brought for the presentation night ('just in case she won', she'd told him) hanging on the back of the door. For a while he sat motionless on the bed. Finally he left the room, walked over to the communal dining room and found Nada making breakfast.

She was talking to me but I can't remember a lot of what she said. I just remember there were a couple of other people there and they started talking about Sue and her being dead. At some point it must have got to me because I got up and shouted, 'It's not fair, we've only been married a year', and I hit the wall as hard as I could.

The thing was, I really didn't believe Sue was dead and everyone around me was talking like she was. It was like no one believed in her and I was just stuck there with them not able to do anything.

I went back down to the beach at some point and I sat on my own for a long time just looking at the sea. You could see it was rough out there. The wind was really blowing and when you looked at it you knew it was going to be so much worse offshore where Sue was. I'd think, 'They're right, this is the third day. How can anyone, after two days swimming, survive in that?' But I'd say that in one breath and in the next I'd say, 'Well, Sue's a really good swimmer and really determined and what can I do to help her?'

I remember the sun starting to go down and walking back up the hill with a few people. They wanted me to go up the pub. I can't remember much about the pub, just that I didn't want to be there. I had a beer and said I had to go.

Late that afternoon Sue noticed the wind shifting around Erskine Island, whipping up tiny particles of sand from the beach and firing them in the direction of her camp. She didn't feel much like moving — it had taken a long time to find a comfortable spot out of the sun. But she sensed the wind was only going to get stronger so she crawled out from her hollow and started to gather up her things.

I was very weak and I couldn't walk very far without my stick but I knew I had to find a new camp before it got dark. It took a couple of trips for me to carry all my stuff around but I got there eventually. The good thing was, the wind cooled things down a bit so after I had a bit of a rest I decided to tackle the turtle hollow again. I can't say the rest made it any easier. Looking back on it now I have to say I admire the turtles and how they lay their eggs — it's quite ingenious. But that wasn't what I thought at the time.

I must have dug away at that hollow for a good two hours — I got down a fair way too. I hit wet sand on a few occasions and started thinking, 'I must be close', but then the dry sand from the sides would fold back into the hole and I'd have to dig that out. That happened again and again and each time it happened I felt myself getting more and more frustrated. I really felt like walking away but I told myself this was the only food source and I had to keep trying. But it didn't seem to matter what I did or how logical I was, the hole seemed structurally designed to stop this sort of attempt. In the end, it all got a bit too much so I decided to leave it and try again later.

My main concern was water. I was pretty much sure someone would see me soon and all I had to do was just conserve my energy until then. I remember it getting cooler and putting on my skivvy and trying to put my wetsuit on again to keep warm and then sitting up on the beach and watching the sunset. I can remember thinking a lot about Greg and I suppose if I learned anything from what I'd been through, it was how much he meant to me. But when I really think back to that night, the main thing I remember is this huge sense of relief — just looking out over the reef at the sea and feeling safe.

The next thing I remember is looking out from the hollow and it was getting lighter. Just looking at the sky I knew it was going to be another hot day. I picked up my little container and realized there was hardly any water left and I lay there for a while wondering what on earth I was going to do.

The Tannum Sands Hotel sits at the top of a hill with a wide, uninterrupted view of the ocean. But Merv Sheehan wasn't there to appreciate the view: in fact he didn't care where they went that evening. What mattered was that they, the spearos, gathered to pay their respects. The last thing he expected was trouble.

The public bar was packed with spearos. Greg and Merv were sitting at a table with the four juniors, the gentle giant Les Gleeves and Blabster. Merv didn't pay much attention to anyone — he just stared at his beer, big tears rolling down his face.

'It wasn't a game any more', says Mark. 'Merv was crying and Greg, he was as white as a ghost.'

'It started to dawn on us what was really happening', says Vlado. 'That we had really lost her.'

Greg had a single beer and left. Shortly after that the men became aware of a stranger speaking loudly at the bar. He claimed to be a local trawlerman and he was highly critical of the spearos. Two beers later and he was standing at their table, claiming they were all responsible for Sue's death, or as good as — they had left her to die. On any other night Merv would have written him off as a drunken fool and continued with his beer, but this was no ordinary night.

'It wasn't a fight. It was one push from Merv', says Lennie. 'And he flew away', says Mark, drawing a wide crescent with his arm. 'He landed on this table and chairs: CRASH! I just couldn't believe you could get so much momentum in those stocky little arms.'

Merv was totally oblivious to the sudden hush in the bar and the looks of amazement on the others' faces. The main thing on his mind was that the man's head had landed near the exit door and the car park was all gravel. 'I didn't expect him to get up but he did and he ran through the car park, which would have been 100 metres long, in bare feet. I never saw him again.'

RESCUE

We all failed Sue. She saved herself.

Andy Ruddock

In 1983, there were three Bell Jetrangers based at Gladstone Airport, all property of Lloyd Helicopters and primarily used to carry guests on the thirty-minute panoramic flight to and from Heron Island Resort. Officially, Lloyds were not involved in the search for Sue Dockar. Unofficially, pilot and manager David Hogan and Heron Resort manager Brian Edmonds had been searching since the first day.

'Normally we don't become involved unless someone officially authorizes the flight and is prepared to pay for it. On this occasion I elected to conduct an aerial search, with Brian as observer', says David Hogan.

Late on the first evening the two men flew low over the sea following the reef line and the run of the tide. They searched until dark, then for some twenty minutes after, using the helicopter landing lights. But a low-level sea search is a dangerous game, particularly at night in a helicopter not equipped for that task. In the end the risk grew too great so they flew back to Heron Island.

On the second day both men were up at first light. In the hour or so before David's first scheduled flight they again flew low over the reefs and islands — all to no avail.

'Searching for a person in the water is very difficult', he says.

It's a bit like looking out in a field and trying to spot a rabbit. It is there, but you try and pick it out ... If it moves you've got more chance of spotting it. And obviously, a person in the water — if they wave their arms you've got a better chance of spotting them. But if there's whitecaps then it is more difficult.

David Hogan had four flights scheduled to Heron that day and the other two Lloyd pilots had a similar number. Between them they agreed to fly wide of their normal route, keeping an eye out for Sue and encouraging their passengers to do likewise. But despite their best efforts and numerous false alarms no one spotted Sue.

By the third day he was looking for a body, although secretly he had lost hope of finding her at all. But he had given his word he'd keep searching, so until the police said otherwise that was what he would do.

It was 5 January 1983 — day four. At 6.30 am David Hogan departed Gladstone Airport for Heron Island with four passengers on board. He smiled and greeted his passengers as usual, but unlike the previous three days he did not advise them about the search. 'I didn't think it appropriate to have them start their holiday by looking for a body on their scenic flight over the Great Barrier Reef.'

Despite time constraints he flew well south of the direct route to Heron, with the intention of doing a similar sweep north on the return journey. He looked straight down, scanning the relatively small area below the helicopter.

'It's much easier to sight a body in the water than a person. A body will lie horizontal whereas a live person tends to be vertical in the water with only the head really showing.'

When he first noticed a lone figure on the beach at Erskine Island he dismissed the sighting as 'just someone off a passing boat'. Then he looked again and realized there was no boat to be seen. 'I reasoned it was out of sight on the north side of the island.' Nevertheless, he made a mental note to check it out on the return flight. At 7.10 am he dropped his passengers at Heron Island and took off alone.

As it started to heat up I took my wetsuit off again and went for a walk around the island checking every container I came across just in case I'd missed one the previous day or the tide had carried something new in. I was very aware that without water I could only survive on the island for a couple more days at most. I knew the only way I could survive longer was to go back into the lagoon and try and catch a fish.

At that point I'd pretty much decided I was going to get my gun and try and spear a fish. I wasn't looking forward to it at all but I knew that was what I had to do. I'd just about talked myself into it when I heard a noise. I turned around and that's when I saw the helicopter coming towards the island.

I was standing there holding onto my stick for support but as it started getting closer and closer I started waving frantically. I waved so much I nearly fell over. It was getting so close and I thought, 'You've got to see me! Please, you've just got to see me!' I could hardly believe it when the helicopter started coming down. I could see the pilot and I realized he was looking at me. He raised his hand up for me to stay back and I knew he was going to land on the island. That was quite a moment for me. I knew it was all over and I was going to be OK. I'm not an emotional person but when that helicopter landed I just fell down on my knees in thanks. The pilot got out of his helicopter and helped me up. He said, 'Are you Sue Dockar?' and I said 'Yes'.

Greg Dockar had walked back from the Tannum Sands Hotel in the dark. It wasn't far and he welcomed the opportunity to be alone. He knew everyone was trying to do the right thing by him. Going down the pub, holding a wake, that was just their way of dealing with things. But Greg didn't believe Sue was dead.

Nada was waiting for him when he arrived back at Tanyella. The pair sat on the verandah and talked.

Somewhere in that conversation she told me the search had been called off and the safety boats had been sent back to Gladstone. I couldn't believe it. I wanted to talk to Ralph because I just couldn't believe he'd given up on Sue. Nada was trying to calm me down saying I'd have to wait until morning because all the boats had tied up behind *Reefseeker* and the crews were staying there for the night. Nada told me I had to get some rest and that she'd take me over to *Reefseeker* in the morning.

For me, that was the lowest point. I lay there for most of the night. In the morning I was still lying there wide awake so I got up, found the car keys and got in the car. I went into Gladstone, down to the wharf where *Reefseeker* had been tied up the night before. I remember driving down there and if someone was watching they must have thought I was mad because I came boring along the road and screeching round the corner and there was the boat ramp and it probably looked as if I was going to go shooting down the ramp.

I pulled up and I'm looking around thinking, 'Where's the bloody boat?' Of course it was low tide — it had dropped so much I couldn't see the boat at first. I went on board and found Ralph, Tim and the others. Ralph was lying on the edge of the bunk holding his head and — I don't know what he'd been drinking — but oh God he smelled. I said, 'Well, where do you think she is?' And he's going, 'I wish they'd listen to me. I wish they'd listen to me'. He said, 'Oh Greg, she'll come back to the island. I keep telling them'. He was really distressed that no one would listen to him, you know. I said, 'Well I'm listening, I believe you'. I knew if Sue was there then it was the last chance I had to get her back so I figured I'd go down to the airport and hire a helicopter.

I came off *Reefseeker* and I was walking up the road to my car and the police come along and said, 'Are you Greg Dockar?' I said, 'Yes'. They took the car keys off me and told me they were taking me down the cop station for my own good. Apparently Nada had phoned them and told them I'd gone missing.

Anyway I'm sitting there at the cop station and a telephone call came through. I'm sitting there and the guy hangs up and says, 'Ah, they've found your wife'. Just like a matter of course, like, 'The sun's come up today'. I said, 'Dead or alive?' He said, 'Alive'.

Then I broke down.

PARTY

Spearos like to think they're pretty tough, but none of them had done what Sue had done and most of them knew they would have died trying.

Ray Inkpen

It was a little after eight in the morning when the office telephone rang. Not that Ray Inkpen knew or cared about the time. 'Manslaughter' — the unlawful killing of another without intent to kill — that was the charge Ray had been told he might face. Merv had told him not to worry: 'It's all talk', he'd said. 'We'll fight the bastards.' But that word, that prospect, had dominated Ray's thoughts ever since.

Ray had not attended the wake — he didn't feel he had the right to be there. Instead, he had risen after a restless sleep and headed over to the office — the sooner all the paperwork was attended to, the sooner he could get the comp over and done with and he and Helen could go home. As for the ringing phone, it was only going to be more bad news — another reporter, more questions from the police, a relative wanting to know what had happened and why.

But whoever it was they were most persistent. In the end he reluctantly answered the call.

> It was Greg Dockar. He was, well, for want of a better term, he was a babbling idiot. He was saying, 'They've found Sue, they've found Sue, you've got to go out and tell them, Sue's alive!' He kept saying it over and over. I couldn't work out if he was drunk or what and at first it didn't click what he was going on about. Then I realized what he was saying.
> He said he was going out to the airport to meet her. I went outside and yelled out as loud as I could: 'They've found Sue! She's alive!'

Dormitory doors flew open and half dressed, hungover men stumbled out onto the verandahs, whooping and cheering. Then Ray went to the communal dining room.

> I walked in there and shouted out again that Sue was alive. A lot of people were really, really happy and all they wanted to know was if Sue was OK and when they could see her. But there were a bunch of guys in there sitting around a table and you know what, they didn't look up from their breakfast.

He had once called them friends. He left the kitchen and walked back towards the office. Cheers and shouts of 'She's alive!' reverberated around Tanyella. The first car loads of spearos were already heading into Gladstone. Ray Inkpen went back to the office and shut the door.

The helicopter flight from Erskine Island to Gladstone Airport took approximately twenty-five minutes. Sue Dockar sat in the front seat next to David.

It was quite strange really: all that time in the water I'd been counting away the minutes and all of a sudden I was in the helicopter and everything was moving very quickly. I knew I was going to be in Gladstone in no time and I started feeling quite apprehensive — sort of like on that first day when I got swept out. I don't know why. I suppose at the back of my mind I was worried what reception I was going to get because I knew me being missing would have caused a lot of trouble.

I didn't know David's name at that point. I could hear him talking on the radio. I think he called head office or something and told them we were coming in. I remember asking him if he had anything to drink. He said not in the cockpit and told me to hang in there, we'd be back in Gladstone soon. Then I looked down as we came over Masthead Island and I saw a turtle swimming near the reef. I knew its carapace would be a good metre across. I said, 'How high are we?' I think David said 1000 feet and I looked down at the turtle again and realized it was just this black dot in the water. Suddenly it dawned on me just how small and insignificant I would have been from the air and how difficult I would have been to spot. Even my HELP signs that I'd thought were so big would have barely been visible. I turned to David to tell him this but he nodded and put his fingers to his lips, signalling that I shouldn't talk, and I realized how croaky my voice must sound. For the rest of the trip I sat back and took in the view.

The next thing you know we're coming in to land. I saw Greg standing there with the police. I was very excited and I was waving to him from the helicopter. I desperately wanted to get out and hold him but I had to wait for the rotor blades to stop. As soon as they stopped Greg came running across the tarmac. He pulled the door open and we just hugged each other. There were tears streaming down his face. Then he went to pick me up but his arms caught the cuts on the back of my legs and I screamed so he put me back down.

There was an ambulance there and Greg wanted the guys to come and get me but I wanted to walk. It is hard for me to explain why, but it was very important to me at the time. I knew people were looking at me and I wanted them to know I was OK, that I'd made it on my own and I could stand on my own two feet.

I walked over to the ambulance and sat on the bed. The ambos told me to lie down but I didn't want to. I sat up for the whole trip. I remember being put on a trolley at the hospital and someone wheeling me along a corridor. I remember bright lights and then Merv's face looking down at me and him saying, 'Thank Christ, Sue'. I kept asking for a drink.

I really didn't want to be in hospital at all. Everyone was very nice and everything but I didn't feel ill, just like I needed to rest and to get cleaned up a bit. I found all the attention and questions a bit hard to deal with. The worst thing was when the nurses were trying to put an intravenous needle into my arm. It felt like I was being stabbed with a stiletto; the pain was excruciating. Then I heard one of them saying, 'You're not going to find it, her veins have collapsed', so they tried my other hand, which again felt like they were putting a stiletto through it. I thought, 'Why are they doing this? It's worse being here in hospital than floating about in the sea'.

At some point they took me to have a bath and I finally got to look in a mirror. I looked awful. My hair was bleached white and my face was badly burned and there were blisters all over my face and lips. I'd lost skin where my mask had been rubbing, particularly under my nose and on my forehead. I knew it would get better eventually so I'd just have to put up with it for now. The thing that bothered me most at the time was my hair — it was a real mess and I asked for some shampoo and conditioner but there wasn't any. I don't know why it bothered me because in the general scheme of things it wasn't a big deal. But what I really wanted more than anything was to wash my hair.

A bit later they took me into a room and started to dress the sores on the back of my legs. I was lying on my stomach and one of the nurses — she'd just transferred over from the burns unit at Rockhampton Hospital — she was checking out the cuts on the backs of my legs. I just remember Greg standing there and looking worried and then I realized it had all gone very quiet in the room. She kept asking me if I felt anything. I kept saying no, no, that's alright. I didn't know what the matter was. Then all of a sudden I felt this stabbing pain in my leg and cried out. It really hurt but everybody seemed quite relieved. Later on Greg told me they had to dig down a fair way before I felt anything.

At the time I didn't know what had been going on with the search or what Greg and Merv had been through. I just remember the two of them sitting next to the bed. They both looked very tired and Greg looked like he hadn't shaved for a few days but they looked really happy. They started to ask me what had happened and I started to tell them and then I realized Merv was crying. He had a big smile on his face and he was saying, 'What a great effort!' but he was crying and so I leaned over and I gave him a hug. I suppose that's when I stopped worrying about how people were going to react. I had Greg and Merv with me and I knew I was going to be OK.

The staff at Gladstone District Hospital were well acquainted with the sudden, often frantic influx of friends and relatives following an emergency admission. What was unusual in this instance was the number. There had been a steady stream of visitors all morning — mainly men, some carrying flowers, many clearly nursing hangovers, all of them asking for Sue Dockar. At one point so many people arrived that the nurses had to split them into shifts but no one complained, least of all Sue. Apart from the deep wounds behind her knees, coral cuts, sunburn and dehydration she was in remarkably good shape. As she told people repeatedly that day, she felt very lucky, very privileged to be alive.

Greg Dockar has vivid memories of those hours.

> I didn't know you could go through so many emotions in the one day. You could say I felt ecstatic, yet at the same time I felt emotionally drained, like I'd been through a war.
>
> The main thing I remember is the looks on people's faces when they walked into the room. I mean, Sue wasn't a pretty sight. There were blisters on her mouth and face, and where the mask was her skin wasn't there anymore and people were just looking at her aghast.
>
> I remember one bunch came in and it was as if they were in shock. None of them knew what to say so they were just staring at her with their mouths open. Then someone piped up and said, 'It was a three-day comp Sue, not three days in a row', and everyone started laughing.
>
> I just sat next to Sue most of the time, just holding her hand and listening to her. She wasn't making a big deal of anything, she was just sitting there in bed telling it how it was. I'd been telling them all this time that Sue was tough and she was still alive but when you listened to her talk, well, I think that's when people realized just how tough she was.

Officially the party at Tanyella kicked off around lunchtime. It didn't matter that Sue wasn't there in person — three days of rumour and grim speculation were swept aside by her hospital bed accounts of pitch-black seas, hallucinations and the far-off sounds of dogs howling in the night. 'It was like she'd risen from the dead', says Blabster.

By late afternoon relief, jubilation and free flowing beer had the safety boat crews elevated to hero status. Fuel consumption and chart references later indicated that over the previous three days they had searched around 1000 square kilometres of open sea, twelve small islands and some eight to ten reefs.

As for the Masthead Island castaways, their time on the island, the mutton birds, the cricket match on the beach, Peter Inskip's gunpowder chowder were already growing into spearfishing legend. But the biggest cheer that afternoon came when Ralph finally arrived. He accepted the accolades with good grace and typical humour. But as the evening wore on those around him saw just how hard the last three days had been on him. 'I've never seen anyone look so worn out yet still be upright', says one spearo who was there. 'I think Sue surviving and turning up just where he said she would, well it justified everything he'd said and done.'

Within hours of Sue's rescue, her story was headline news. Pictures of 'Miracle Survivor Sue Dockar', her 'tired but clearly jubilant husband' and 'hero pilot David Hogan' were beamed around Australia. Newspaper reports described her as 'iron-willed', a 'survival heroine', 'Australia's bravest skindiver'.

But not everyone accepted Sue's account.

Sergeant Cooper and Senior Constable Perkins were still at Heron Island when the news first broke. Within half an hour, the two officers along with two staff from the resort were en route to Erskine Island.

'The report was that she didn't look as weather-beaten and as much distressed as they thought she would have been if she had been in the water for the length of time she claimed', says Neville Cooper.

Something else bothered him. The previous day, the day Sue Dockar 'claimed', as he put it, to have been thrown over Erskine

Reef, he and Senior Constable Perkins had circumnavigated the island in the police launch.

> We'd done a circuit of Erskine Island that particular morning, and we'd done a circuit of Erskine and Masthead Island that particular afternoon and there was no sign of her, no sight of her.
>
> There was no thought of going ashore to search the island because that had already been done. You could say that was a mistake, we should have searched the island again. But how many times do you search an island? And what are the chances of getting washed back up on the same island you literally got washed away from, particularly when you think how long she was in the water and where she would have travelled? The chances of being washed back up on that same island were so remote.

Then there were Greg Dockar's assertions that his wife was a strong swimmer, capable of swimming long distances. Neville doesn't say who came up with the theory, just that somehow, someone suggested:

> … she, in cahoots with her husband, may have swum to Masthead Island, stayed there for a couple of days and swum back to Erskine Island with a view of selling her story and making a bit of money on it. Far fetched, but nevertheless we had to run that out.

They searched Erskine Island for anything that might confirm or deny Sue's story. They found nothing. Sue was later interviewed by Gladstone Police, at the time totally unaware she was under suspicion. Her story did not vary.

So when all is said and done, does Neville Cooper believe her?

To plan something like that takes cunning, particularly in a remote area. It would be different if you had been there before and you could calculate it and say, 'Yeah, we can do this'. She hadn't and that takes away from the theory. But the theory was certainly put forward. In the end there was no evidence to support it so we can only assume that everything she claimed happened, happened — and that's certainly a feat of great endurance if it's true, really a miracle that she survived in the condition she did. We can put that down to her strength and endurance in the water. And certainly, mentally she had to be very strong to be able to last that long.

Sue never met Sergeant Cooper or his offsider. When the search was over they headed straight back to Yeppoon. She gave a statement to Gladstone Police and as far as Sue was concerned that was the end of the matter. All she wanted was to get out of hospital.

I couldn't relax. I'd heard the news reports that evening and I found myself going over and over what had happened and the fact that I'd survived. Up until then it hadn't really dawned on me that it was such a big thing.

I didn't sleep much at all mainly because of the pain from the IV. I knew it hadn't been put in right but they told me it was a regular pain. Finally one of the nurses took it out and went, 'Oh man', because it was half in the flesh. My legs were swollen too.

The next morning they gave me scrambled eggs for breakfast. They were really salty and it hurt my lips. Greg came in a little later and I told him I wanted to go. The doctor came over and said I should stay a bit longer but I didn't want to be there any more.

All I wanted was to be with my friends.

EPILOGUE

If Sue had walked away from spearfishing, if she had thrown away her dive gear and vowed never to go near the sea again, a great many people would have understood. She didn't. Just three weeks after discharging herself from hospital Sue was back in the water competing in the Sydney Spearfishing Championships. She admits to being nervous, but not through any fear of the sea. 'There were a lot of people there and I felt like everyone's eyes were on me', she explains.

She gave little away. The quiet but powerful message emanating from Sue was that life was back to normal. Those around her soon fell into step. Merv was already doing what he did best — telling everybody else what to do. The four NSW juniors were enjoying their last week of freedom. Scottie, Mark and Lennie would soon return to school to complete their Higher School Certificates. Vlado was about to take up an apprenticeship. For everyone else it was back to work, bills and domestic chores, back to fishing at the weekends and renovating their homes when they could.

The stares and questions gradually waned and eventually Sue was able to ease herself back to where she was most comfortable in life — just a face in the crowd. At the time those around her interpreted this as 'typical Sue' — modest, 'not wanting to make a fuss'. But there was another reason for her reticence.

It happened after I left hospital. Greg and I went back to Tannum Sands and everyone was there. People were coming up and hugging me and smiling. Someone got me a chair and someone else handed me a beer. They seemed genuinely pleased to see me. But there were a few — it was weird — they wouldn't even speak to me. Then I started to think again about how far they'd come and how much money they would have spent to get to the comp and because of me it was called off. After that I started to look around, wondering what everyone else was really thinking, whether they were just being polite. A little later I found out how much the search cost and that the AUF had been asked to foot the bill. It was all sorted out eventually but from then on it didn't matter what Greg or anyone else said, I came away from Queensland feeling guilty about all the trouble I'd caused. I just wanted to forget the whole thing.

Sue's survival wasn't enough to make everything OK for Ray Inkpen either. After he returned home he systematically packed up, gave away or destroyed anything that reminded him of that fateful competition. 'After that I didn't talk about it, I didn't think about it. I never wanted to dive another spearfishing comp again.'

For ten years Ray stayed completely away from competitive spearfishing. But his love for the sea was still there, and during that time friends had coaxed him back for social dives and the occasional trip away. In 1993 he moved down to Sydney. When he arrived it seemed only natural to call Merv and ask if he wanted to catch up for a dive. They agreed to meet at Merv's house and then launch the boat from Gunnamatta Bay.

I knew Merv and Sue were good mates and given we had a lot of friends in common, chances were I'd bump into her somewhere along the track. But I got the shock of my life when I went around the next day and she was standing there. All those years I'd thought she must hate me for what happened, but she didn't. She shook my hand and asked me how I was. I couldn't help myself. I told her I was sorry for everything that happened but she just smiled at me and said there was nothing to be sorry for.

Sue had no idea of the burden she lifted with those few words.

'I've never blamed anyone for what happened', says Sue, recalling her meeting with Ray.

> The main thing I remember about that day is the water was clear and at some point I dived down and shot a big bream. I was pulling it out from under a rock ledge when I felt this presence behind me. I turned around and saw Ray a few metres away. He gave me the 'OK' signal and I signalled 'OK' back, then we carried on fishing.

It was late January 1998 when Sue first heard the news: a massive air and sea search was under way for two divers missing off the north Queensland coast. She turned up the car radio. Fifteen minutes later came a second, more detailed report. Scuba divers Thomas and Eileen Lonergan from Baton Rouge, Louisiana were among a group of twenty-six divers aboard MV *Outer Edge*. They were last seen entering the water at Fish City, a well-known dive site some 70 kilometres off the north Queensland coast. *Outer Edge* left Fish City at 3.30 pm on 25 January — the skipper unaware the Lonergans were still in the water. It was not until late evening on the 27th that he reported the matter to the police.

Sue switched the radio off. From that point on she paid little attention to media coverage of the Lonergan disappearance. 'It was morbid speculation and I didn't like it', she says.

> People assumed that I'd feel strongly about what happened to the Lonergans, but I can't say I did. My initial thought was: 'How could they have been left behind like that? How could the skipper turn for home without being sure everyone was on board?' I think like most people I found it very sad and disturbing but I didn't feel any empathy. I wish I could say I did, but I didn't.

It would have been different if they were spearos. There's so few of us that if someone goes missing you either know them personally or know of them through friends, so it affects you. The Lonergans, they were scuba divers, tourists. And they were left to die by strangers. That's a totally different scenario to what happened to me.

What did bother me was all that talk at the inquest about them being eaten by sharks and so-called experts saying sharks were attracted by even tiny drops of blood in the water — that's complete crap. I was in the water for two days straight. I saw sharks on the first day when I had fish on my rig and that was it. To me, that type of comment was cruel and unnecessary. All it would have done was caused their families a great deal of pain.

I still remember the dream I had the second night I was in the water and how peaceful it felt and how easy it would have been to do what the voice was telling me — just let go of my buoy and swim down to that little village. I like to think that's what happened to the Lonergans — at some point, they would have just fallen asleep and that would have been it.

But there was another incident that did touch Sue. It took place hundreds of kilometres from the sea, a few months before the Lonergans disappeared. On 30 July 1997, a landslide swept away two ski lodges in the alpine village of Thredbo, killing eighteen people and trapping loan survivor Stuart Diver in freezing mud between two massive concrete slabs. He was entombed for sixty-five hours with his dead wife by his side. The sheer scale of the tragedy and the monumental effort to free Stuart commanded Sue's attention for three days. When he was finally lifted out from under the rubble she found herself close to tears.

When I saw his face and heard everyone cheering as he was carried down the hill I remembered how I felt when I came over the reef and realized I was going to be OK. I remembered the sense of relief and how good it felt to be alive. It was the first time I'd felt any connection or related what happened to me to another person. A few days later, I heard him being interviewed and totally related to how he put his fears and emotions to one side and coped. It was very moving for me.

The other big thing was the paramedic who stayed with him during the rescue — Paul Featherstone. He used to come out spearfishing with us before he joined the elite paramedic squad and started jumping out of helicopters. He always reckoned diving with us toughened him up for the job. Paul crawled into that hole and stayed with Stuart right up until the moment Stuart was carried out. That's what spearos do and that's what Ralph and the other guys did for me. They never gave up; they didn't leave me out there to die. The only reason they went back to shore was because they were ordered to.

I think that's when my perspective started to change. Up until then I felt that when anyone talked about what happened at Erskine all the attention was focused on me and how I survived and that always made me uncomfortable. I'd never had the courage to ask anyone what happened to them during the comp. It took a few years but the more I heard, the more I realized it wasn't just me who got caught out — just about everybody got into trouble. And I gradually started to accept that I hadn't stuffed up and that what happened wasn't my fault. That's when I started thinking seriously about going back to Erskine.

It is late August 2006. Greg is driving Sue to the airport. As he drives she reminds him there are a week's meals in the freezer and their two sons, Paul and Stephen, are meeting up with friends from high school that evening. There's a pile of washing that needs to go in the dryer and the dog needs a walk. Greg nods but Sue is unsure how much he's absorbed. When they pull into the airport drop-off zone, Greg takes off his watch and straps it to her wrist.

'You take care', he says.

'I'll call you when I get there. Love you', says Sue, and she kisses him goodbye.

'Only a few people knew where I was going', says Sue.

> That was the way I wanted it. Greg and I, we'd talked it through a few times over the years — about going back to Erskine. He fully supported me but it's a hard place to get to and we had the mortgage to pay and two young children. There wasn't much left over for luxuries like trips away. And for a long time I couldn't see the point — you know, what it would achieve? That started to change as the kids got older and I found out more about what happened to everyone else during the comp.

The day Sue Dockar boarded the launch to Heron Island, a cool mist shrouded the ocean and the surface of the sea was like glass. She stayed at the gunwale for the entire trip, watching the colour of the water change and the flying fish leap.

Her plan had been to stay at Heron Island overnight and travel to Erskine the next day on one of the resort dive boats. 'I'd imagined walking out from the beach and going for a dive', she says. But that night the weather turned. Sue sat alone on the beach staring into the blackness, listening to the wind howl and the waves crashing down onto the reef.

At eight o'clock the following morning she was standing on Heron Island's weather-beaten wharf. Standing next to her was dive boat skipper Alison Grant. The two women were looking out beyond the confines of the harbour, watching a 30 knot nor'east wind peel waves off the surface of the sea.

'We could have walked there yesterday', said Sue.

'The tides are right', said Alison without turning her head. 'I can get you in there if you still want to go.'

They look down to *Wahoo*, a sleek twin-engine vessel used to take resort guests out to more remote fishing and dive sites. Sue looked again at the windswept sea.

'Then we'd better go', she said.

On a half-reasonable sea it takes *Wahoo* around twenty minutes to sprint from Heron Island to Erskine. That morning — with the wind and waves continually pushing the boat south-west — it took close to double that time. And when they finally arrived, Erskine Island looked more akin to a surf beach than the picturesque coral cay Sue had seen the day before.

'It didn't look good', says Sue.

If Alison had turned the boat around and headed back to Heron I would have understood. But she didn't. She turned *Wahoo* hard port and brought us into the lee of Erskine and then over the rim of the lagoon. It was a very gutsy manoeuvre — I think even Ralph would have been impressed. I'm grateful to her because right up until that moment I wasn't sure if I was doing the right thing coming back. As soon as we got into the lagoon it felt right. I looked down and saw the little fish darting away from the bow and the turtles and rays gliding off into the distance. And I remembered what it was like to really appreciate being alive — I mean really appreciate it and love life. It was quite overwhelming.

I wouldn't describe it as a joyful experience but it was a very significant moment for me, as though a big weight had come off my shoulders. Erskine didn't look like the tiny patch of sand I'd seen from the launch the previous day; it looked wild and beautiful like I remembered it. I think the bad weather made the whole experience even more powerful because apart from the direction of the swell, the sea conditions were pretty much the same as when I came ashore in '83. I pointed out to Alison where I'd come over the reef, where the sea was pummeling the coral. It really brought home just how lucky I'd been to make it back at all.

We didn't spend long on the island — just enough time for me to take a look around. The scrub had grown a lot and the sand had moved a bit, but I found where I made my first camp and where I first spotted Masthead Island and realized that I was on Erskine. I even found a little Orchy bottle — but there was no water in it.

I think everybody has an event or a place that defines who they are. I know a lot of people define me by what happened back in 1983 and for a long time I didn't feel good about that. Now I do. Erskine Island will always be part of who I am.

ACKNOWLEDGMENTS

When I started this book I thought I was writing the story of one woman's survival against the odds. How wrong I was. Over the years I have pried into the lives and sifted through the memories and emotions of some forty men and women.

I would like to start by thanking Sue and Greg Dockar and the Australian spearfishing community for their patience, hospitality and stoic endurance of my questions. Special thanks to Keith Brabham, Mark Colys, Vlado Hric, Lennie Goldsmith, Allan Moore, Tim Paulsen, Gunther Pfrengle, Paul Riorden, Andy Ruddock, Merv Sheehan and Paul Welsby for being so generous with their time. I am particularly grateful to Ralph and Anne Whalley who have sat through countless hours of questions about the search, the reef and the currents yet somehow maintained their humour. Special thanks also to Ray Inkpen. It takes courage to speak of things that have caused great pain; even more to trust another to tell the story. Once again, thank you.

Thank you to Neville Cooper for taking the time to explain the challenges and hard decisions he faced back in 1983. Thanks also to David Hogan for speaking to me not just about the rescue, but for explaining the challenges faced by search and rescue teams, particularly those working in remote areas.

Thanks to Dr Adam Smith and Ian Puckeridge, Terry Maas and Bill Silvester for letting me draw on their vast knowledge of diving and competitive spearfishing; to Dr Carl Edmonds and Dr Glenn Singleman for their perspectives on prolonged immersion and dive physiology; and to Paul Featherstone for sharing his extensive knowledge on the mindset of a survivor. Thank you to the staff at Heron Island Resort; particularly Alison Grant and Andrew Handley for making Sue's trip back to Erskine Island a wonderful experience, and to Queensland Parks and Wildlife Service Ranger Alan Hollis for sharing his knowledge on the birds and turtles of the Capricorn Group. Thanks to John Broadbent and Ray Peddersen of Maritime Safety Queensland for their valuable input on tides and tidal movements.

Thanks to my commissioning editor Hazel Flynn for taking on an unknown author and for keeping me on track. Thanks to my editor Desney Shoemark for her encouragement and close scrutiny.

Thank you, Ron Allum for your love, support and encouragement on those days when writing a page felt like climbing the Eiger. Thank you Madelaine and Sophie for your smiles, hugs and kind words. Thank you Dr Joseph MacInnis, Sarah Groenewegen and Peter Beeh for not letting me give up.

But most of all, thank you Sue Dockar. You have taught me many things. Without your strength and will to survive there would be no story.

First published in 2007 by Pier 9, an imprint of Murdoch Books Pty Limited

Murdoch Books Australia
Pier 8/9
23 Hickson Road
Millers Point NSW 2000
Phone: +61 (0) 2 8220 2000
Fax: +61 (0) 2 8220 2558
www.murdochbooks.com.au

Murdoch Books UK Limited
Erico House, 6th Floor
93–99 Upper Richmond Road
Putney, London SW15 2TG
Phone: +44 (0) 20 8785 5995
Fax: +44 (0) 20 8785 5985
www.murdochbooks.co.uk

Chief Executive: Juliet Rogers
Publishing Director: Kay Scarlett

Commissioning Editor: Hazel Flynn
Design concept: Reuben Crossman
Design: Heather Menzies
Project Manager and Editor: Desney Shoemark
Production: Maiya Levitch

National Library of Australia Cataloguing-in-Publication Data
Allum, Yvette.
        The lonely sea.

        ISBN 9781921208966 (pbk.).

        1. Dockar, Sue. 2. Survival after airplane accidents,
        shipwrecks, etc. - Queensland. 3. Spear fishing -
        Queensland. I. Title.

        613.69092

A catalogue record for this book is available from the British Library.

Printed by i-Book Printing Ltd in 2007. PRINTED IN CHINA.
Reprinted 2008.